"A readable, persuasive overview"

"This is a readable, persuasive overview which should convince us all that God's mission today includes the ministry of earthkeeping. When the Bible says that 'God so loved the world . . . ,' this points us not only to God's love for all people, but to the reach of God's love to all creation. In view of the "groaning of creation" now so evident, the task of mission in the twenty-first century must include outreach which extends God's healing love to the wounds of the earth."

Wesley Granberg-Michaelson
Secretary General, Reformed Churches of America

"Points the way to a full response"

"Points the way to a full response to God's creative, sustaining and redemptive work in the world through missionary earthkeeping."

Calvin B. DeWitt
Director, Au Sable Institute
Professor of Environmental Studies,
University of Wisconsin, Madison

"Prophetically pointing to a new and expanded frontier"

"At last we are moving beyond neglect of the state of the world and recognizing the stewardship responsibilities of our Judeo-Christian tradition . . . This MARC publication is indeed prophetically pointing to a new and expanded frontier of the mission of the church in the twenty-first century."

C. Dean Freudenberger
Professor, Luther Northwestern Theological Seminary
St. Paul, Minnesota

Patching God's Garment

Environment and Mission in the 21st Century

W. Dayton Roberts

121 East Huntington Drive
Monrovia, California
91016-3400 USA

919 West Huntington Drive
Monrovia, California
91016 USA

PATCHING GOD'S GARMENT
Environment and Mission in the 21st Century

W. Dayton Roberts

ISBN 0-912552-85-9

Published by MARC, a division of World Vision International, 121 East Huntington Drive, Monrovia, California 91016-3400, U.S.A.

Printed in the United States of America. Editor and interior page design: Edna G. Valdez. Cover illustration: Brad Eberhard. Cover design: Hearken Creative Services.

This interior of this book is printed on recycled paper.

World Vision's 44 year experience of caring for the world's poor and their children has led us to the recognition that environmental degradation, if left unchecked, will in fact become a poverty issue. The God we worship, the one who created order out of chaos, the one who provided the opportunity of eternal salvation, also cares for the poor.

Children are the reason World Vision, as a Christian organization, exists. They are the central focus of our ministry. Often the best and most effective way to assist children is to look at the impact that their natural environment has on their well-being.

World Vision has been directly involved with environmental concerns in its development work for over ten years. With the tragic events of the 1984 famine in Africa, World Vision began to look at its programs through a different lens. It became evident that so much more could be done for starving children beyond emergency relief feeding centers. World Vision continued to broaden its vision of helping poor and hungry children by examining ways to assist entire communities to produce food for their own children.

In doing so, World Vision began to look at the environmental impact that depleted natural resources had on a community's ability to survive unassisted.

World Vision began assisting the children of the Ansokia Valley in Africa and other communities by replenishing the productivity of the land and helping their parents to build a self-sustaining community through restoring permanent clean water sources, reclaiming eroded land through the building of check-dams, planting trees for reforestation, and reviving land for productive farming.

The care of God's creation is an important biblical principle. It is out of our love for God, our commitment to the world's hurting children, and our conviction to follow Jesus that we involve ourselves in caring for God's creation.

World Vision is committed to promoting awareness and understanding of global issues that we believe have an impact on the world's poor and their children. On behalf of World Vision, the Office of Advocacy and Education is happy to introduce this book to the community of Christians who share our commitment for the care and healthy development of the world's children.

Paul Thompson
Vice President, Advocacy and Education

WORLD VISION

919 W. Huntington Drive
Monrovia, California 91016

Contributing Authors

Maurice F. Strong was once called "the custodian of the planet" by the *New York Times*. He was senior executive of the Power Corporation of Canada, and headed up what became the Canadian International Development Agency (CIDA). In the United Nations, Strong served as Under Secretary to Secretary-General U Thant, organized and coordinated two global congresses on the environment (Stockholm in 1972 and Río in 1992), and was founding director of the United Nations Environmental Programme (UNEP), based in Nairobi, Kenya. He is currently chairman of Ontario Hydro, and chairman of the Earth Council, a non-UN body birthed at the Río conference.

Dwayne Hodgson is a Canadian-born graduate student in the field of social theology, with a heart for Christian environmentalism. He received his B.A. and B.S. from McMaster University. He has worked with InterVarsity Christian Fellowship in Lithuania, as a volunteer at ECO-ED (World Congress on Education and Communication on Environment & Development), and for McMaster's Theme School on International Justice and Human Rights. His future plans include theological studies, freelancing as a photojournalist and teaching at the university level.

Ronald J. Sider is professor of theology and culture at Eastern Baptist Theological Seminary in Wynnewood, Pennsylvania. He is president of Evangelicals for Social Action, which has recently taken a lead role in launching the Evangelical Environmental Network. Co-sponsored by World Vision, the EEN is a national organization committed to nurturing a biblically grounded environmental movement in the evangelical community. Sider is a graduate of Yale University with an M.A. and Ph. D. in history. He is author of numerous books and articles, the best-known of which is *Rich Christians in an Age of Hunger.* His most recent book is *One-sided Christianity? Uniting the Church to Heal a Lost and Broken World* . Sider has recently been named as corresponding editor for *Christianity Today.*

Stephen K. Commins is director of policy and planning at World Vision International. His work includes relations with international organizations, strategic planning and public policy issues. He has a Ph. D. in regional planning from UCLA and was director of the Development Institute at the UCLA African Studies Center for seven years. Dr. Commins is the author of two dozen articles and chapters on development-related topics. He served for six years on the board of directors of Bread for the World, and was recently elected to the board of Global Tomorrow Coalition, an organization with business, environmental and development members.

Job Ebenezer is director of the Environmental Stewardship and Hunger division of the Evangelical Lutheran Church in America. He was director of correctional education at Las Lunas Correctional Center, New Mexico, and an instructor in engineering at the New York Institute of Technology and the University of New Mexico. Ebenezer is a graduate of the University of Madras, the Indian Institute of Science and Stevens Institute of Technology (Ph. D., mechanical engineering). He serves on the board of trustees of the Au Sable Institute for Environmental Studies, of Servants in Faith and Technology, and of the North American Conference on Christianity and Ecology. Ebenezer is also the author of a number of articles in professional and popular publications.

William A. Dyrness is dean of the School of Theology and professor of theology and culture at Fuller Theological Seminary in Pasadena, California. He received bachelor's degrees from Wheaton College and Columbia Theological Seminary, a B. Div. from Fuller and his D. Theol. from the University of Strasbourg, France. In 1976, he received the doctorandus from Free University, Amsterdam, and conducted additional post-doctoral work at Cambridge University. He has served overseas as a missionary and professor at Asian Theological Seminary in Manila, Philippines, and in Nairobi, Kenya, and was president and professor at New College, Berkely, California, before assuming his present position.

Contents

. . . the earth shall wear out like a garment.
Isaiah 51:6

Lord, in the beginning you made the earth,
and the heavens are the work of your hands.
They will disappear into nothingness,
but you will remain forever.
They will become worn out like old clothes,
and some day you will fold them up and replace them.
But you yourself will never change,
and your years will never end.
Hebrews 1:10-12

Acknowledgements

A book like this one could never be prepared and published without utilizing many valuable resources. I am especially grateful to:

The United Nations Environmental Programme (UNEP) for the report it provided to the Brazil (1992) Conference on Environment and Development (UNCED), entitled *Saving Our Planet: Challenges and Hopes*, and Vol. 4, No. 2, of *Our Planet*, the magazine of UNEP.

Dr. Fernando Zumbado, assistant administrator and regional director for Latin America and the Caribbean of the United Nations Development Programme (UNDP), and to his staff, for their report on what happened at the UNCED in Brazil.

Tyndale House Publishers for permission to use extensively the text of *The Living Bible*. Unless otherwise indicated, all Scripture quotations are from *The Living Bible*.

Dr. Maurice Strong, founding director of the UNEP and coordinator of the UNCED, for his helpful Foreword.

Dr. Ronald Sider and Dwayne Hodgson, Drs. Stephen Commins, Job Ebenezer and William Dyrness for the illuminating reactions that they submitted for publication in the closing chapters of this book.

Vice President Al Gore, ecologists Calvin DeWitt, Ghillean Prance, Dennis Testerman, Sandra Postel, Loren Wilkinson, Tony Campolo, Ted Dyrness and others whose writings and lectures were a source of information and encouragement.

John Kenyon, my publisher, and to several members of my family who read parts of the manuscript and encouraged me to complete the project. Particularly to my wife Hilda, who read every word of it, who never ceased to bolster the flagging spirits of its weary author, and who endured in solitary patience his interminable sessions at the word processor.

The Lord God, who gave sparks of insight and inspiration at precisely the right times, and who provided the strength and wisdom necessary for the completion of the task.

W. Dayton Roberts

Foreword
To replenish the earth

Maurice F. Strong

It is often a good idea to go back to square one—to pause and survey critically our position on the great flowchart of history, and to take stock of our successes and our failures. God's instruction to Adam and Eve, as chronicled in the first book of the Old Testament, provides a fundamental bench mark for such an assessment.

On the first and last of the objectives set out in that early mandate, we have certainly outdone ourselves. We have been fruitful and multiplied our species to the point of pre-empting most of the earth's resources.

And we have most assuredly subdued the earth. We have dug deeply into its crusts and removed the substances with which we have not merely survived, but fashioned a way of life undreamed of by past generations. Not only can we circumnavigate the globe in hours, but we can also surmount gravity and vault beyond the earth.

But the biblical injunction was also to "replenish the earth." By this crucial criterion, we must judge ourselves prodigal and profligate.

The evidence of our wasteful and destructive exploitation of the earth has been mounting for some time. This has led to an increasing awareness of the risks this exploitation is posing to the human future. Across the span of my own life, I have heard the solitary voices of environmental pioneers multiply and swell into an international chorus of people committed to protect, conserve and renew our planet's environment. I have dedicated much of my own time and energy over the past two decades to translating these concerns into the practical measures and behavioral changes required to ensure our common future.

But as the Earth Summit held in Río de Janeiro in 1992 made clear, we are still a very long way from accomplishing our goals. Even as we talk about the need for change, our relentless pursuit of gross national product continues to outstrip our efforts to conserve resources. We continue to slip backwards in the struggle for sustainability and quality growth.

Yet the Earth Summit in Río de Janeiro ignited new hope that we may yet make the change of course required to place us on a pathway to a more secure and sustainable future. As a result of an unprecedented ground swell of popular pressure, world leaders agreed on a set of principles, the Declaration of Río, and a practical program to give effect to these principles, Agenda 21, which provide the basis for the change of course on which our future depends.

But this change of course is fundamental in nature and will not come easily. The agreements reached by world leaders at Río represent a necessary and promising starting point. Yet we have learned that agreements by governments are not enough. They must be rooted in and propelled by the sustained commitment and action of a concerned and motivated citizenry. These motivations stem, ultimately, from our deepest spiritual, moral and ethical values.

This is why I dare to hope that the great religions of the world—especially Islam, Judaism and Christianity, which believe in the God of creation—may rise to their responsibilities and empower this movement with the commitment and support of the global communities they represent. I remain convinced that religious conviction, and the disciplined behavior that flows from it, have a unique potential to produce the resolve and motivation required to "replenish the earth."

This is why I welcome *Patching God's Garment*. It is a compelling voice from the respected evangelical wing of Protestantism.

It expresses a cry felt in all perceptive segments of our global family today. Awareness and action, inspired by our faith in God, are the surest path to sustainability and survival.

This book deserves a widespread readership and I particularly commend its contents to the careful attention of all readers.

Toronto, Canada
August 1993

Bottom-shelf ecology

Why is a missionary writing about the environment?

Because as a missionary, I care about the hundreds of thousands of Somalis who are dying of starvation. I also care about the millions who are surviving in an Africa that consumes more food than it produces.

I care about the victims of floods in Bangladesh, and about the subsistence farmers elsewhere who are being impoverished by the spreading swathes of sterile desert, the erosion of land or its salinization.

I feel it to the marrow when I see tropical forests disappearing and learn that humanity's practices threaten the planet's biodiversity and abundance of species, because I know the poverty and disease that these practices exacerbate.

I am grieved by the "africanization" of Haiti's lovely island and the barrenness of Nicaragua's hills.

I am pained most deeply, however, by the indifference of my Christian brothers and sisters—not so much to the suffering I have referred to—but to the despoiling and the devastation of our environment that are causes of this suffering.

Important reasons for concern

There are many reasons why the facts and potential consequences of the environmental crisis should profoundly concern an evangelical missionary—every evangelical missionary. Beyond what I have already mentioned, I see half a dozen important reasons for such concern:

1

1. God entrusted the stewardship of his creation to the human race. As missionaries and "world Christians," we should take the lead in the path of obedience.

   In other words, quoting Calvin DeWitt and Ghillean Prance, "We who bring the good news of God's love for the cosmos (John 3:16) and of Jesus Christ's work as Creator, sustainer and reconciler (John 1; Col. 1; Heb. 1) cannot be complicit bystanders or participants in the degradation and defilement of the world God creates, loves, sustains and reconciles."[1]

2. Some trustworthy thinkers describe our Christian responsibility in even stronger terms. "We are stewards," says missionary theologian Luther Copeland, "but we are more than stewards . . . We are priests who view the world with reverence because it is God's handiwork. We are to represent the creation to God and act toward it according to [God's] attitude and intent."[2]

3. The environmental crisis is concentrated most acutely in the Third World countries of the tropical belt around the globe—the midsections of America, Africa and Asia, a few degrees north and south of the equator. This belt is the home of the planet's biodiversity (in rain forests and coral reefs), the center of its weather machine, and the receptor and circulator of the solar energy that keeps us alive.

   It is also the target of much of our missionary outreach, and therefore an area of special concern to us. It is the part of our globe most lacking in a knowledge of Christ as Lord and Savior. The AD2000 movement calls the Afro-Asian part of this area our "10/40 window" on the unevangelized world. It is urgently in need of the Christian gospel and of some ecological awareness as well.

4. Environmental concerns will be a major focus of theology in the twenty-first century. We must grapple now with the issues they pose—otherwise we will "miss the boat."

   Christian sociologist Tony Campolo suggests that the evangelical Christian church may have lost a generation of young Americans because it was slow to confront civil rights issues in the 1960s.

The same thing could happen with environmental issues, he warns.[3]

5. This is, in part, because environmental deterioration today has replaced nuclear annihilation as the underlying risk and pressure on world affairs. The nations cower together under a new sword of Damocles. In the words of social ethicist J. Mark Thomas,

> New to the contemporary situation is the degradation of the environment that today unites the world by mutual threat. While less dramatic than the nuclear menace, environmental damage contains the quiet peril of destroying the conditions for life on the planet. Because ecological threats have the character of slow strangulation rather than sudden death, they are the more insidious and dangerous. They can be ignored or denied until the planetary victim is beyond help. Powerful economic, political and cultural interests, for the sake of short-term gains, can build temporary refuge from global repercussions until ultimate destruction is inevitable.[4]

6. I see the environmental countdown as the "grandfather's clock" of what the Bible calls the "latter days"—referring, perhaps, to ours and the next generation(s). You remember how the song goes:

> Ninety years without slumbering—
> tick, tock, tick, tock—
> His life seconds numbering—
> tick, tock, tick, tock.
> But it stopped short, never to go again,
> when the old man died.

Environmental overload and the day of reckoning

Scripture seems to indicate that the environment and the human race will face together the destiny of death and resurrection that God has planned for us. If so, the most reliable chronometer of end-time history is the deterioration of the planet's ecosystems.

The current environmental crisis is a potent reminder that our Lord will soon return to bring human history—and the evil it reflects—to its appointed conclusion.

I don't mean that we should disregard other "signs of the times"—the deterioration of social behavior, for example, or the preaching of the gospel to the "whole world, so that all nations will hear it, and then, finally, the end will come" (Matt. 24:14). I simply insist that environmental overload is a clear and measurable gauge of sustainable life on the planet, and that it shows us how close we are to the day of reckoning.

Nearly twenty years ago I published a little book called *Running Out, a compelling look at the current state of Planet Earth.*[5] My thesis was that Planet Earth is rapidly running out of edible food, clean air, potable drinking water and living space. Our small world, I pointed out, is rapidly becoming overpopulated.

"So you're a Christian," the book ventured, "living in the twentieth century on Planet Earth. How are you going to live in a world where everything is running out?"

That was in 1975, when most Christians were not only indifferent to the environmental crisis but were almost totally ignorant of it.

And I'm sure I posed more questions than answers!

At any rate, in its English edition, the book appeared to make little impact, if any, in the U.S. Published in Spanish, however, I believe it possibly made a modest contribution to a new ecological awareness—in Costa Rica, at least, where a unique program of national parks and wildlife preserves has set a hopeful example to the rest of the world.

Environmental awareness has increased dramatically everywhere over the last two decades. To be sure, we have accomplished far too little, but we have realized some progress in conserving our resources, protecting our environment and reducing our waste and pollution.

Naturalists, economists and theologians have written much on related subjects. These writings have not received a fair hearing, however, because many potential readers automatically discount

4

ecological reporting as "New Age," or extremist Greenpeace politicking, or simply sensational fear-mongering.

In any case, population growth is still outstripping overwhelmingly our meager efforts to promote ecological awareness and environmental protection. The writings for our enlightenment in this area are often too scientific, too profound, too complicated. These reports fail to wrestle with several simple problems of the Christian faith and attitude as they touch our past and future, our history and our hope of life to come.

A basic primer of Christian environmentalism

Patching God's Garment, therefore, is an attempt to provide a basic primer of Christian environmentalism. It shows what we need to understand about our ecosystem, God's purposes in human history, the mission of the church, what we can realistically expect to accomplish and how we should direct our social and personal activities and lifestyles.

The book builds its thesis about the Christian and his world on a metaphor of the Old Testament psalmist (Ps. 102:25-27, NIV). David called the earth and the heavens of God's creation ". . . a garment. Like clothing you will change them and they will be discarded," he sang, "but you remain the same, and your years will never end."

The human race, bearing God's image and hosting God incarnate in Jesus Christ, shares this garment with its Creator. We need to care for it, repair it and make it last for as long as God intends it to endure. Stewardship of nature and the environment is implicit in the image of God and explicit in his mandate.

The garment is not eternal nor indestructible. It is wearing out and God will ultimately replace it, but for the present we can patch it up and keep it useful. The God of grace, who promised new life to human believers, also promised "new heavens and a new earth" (Isa. 65:17, NIV). Death and resurrection are intrinsic to this plan. Meanwhile, we are under obligation to keep "patching."

I understand the status of the environment is analogous to that of some of us who are in our declining years. We don't know when, but we know that ultimately we must expect to "cross the Jordan River" from this earthly existence, through death, to the Promised Land of eternal life and joy. Meanwhile, we take care of our health with greater zeal than ever. Quality of life is one of our major concerns.

More than any others, Christians should assume leadership in the field of environmental protection. Instead, they have been slow to develop ecological awareness and are confused about the mission of the church in a new and frightening age of famine and pollution, of exploding populations and vanishing resources.

We need to ask and answer the simple questions: What is the environmental crisis? How does it affect the church's evangelistic imperative and the nature of its ministry? Is there anything we can do? Anything we must do?

That is what we are attempting here. Reading this book will help mission strategists, laymen, pastors and Christian leaders from different backgrounds to define their own paths of obedience.

PART I - BASICS

An Abbreviated Theology of the Environment

1

How the world works . . .
and falters!

Surrounded by flowering bougainvillea and jacaranda, the
United Nations Environmental Programme (UNEP) headquarters
is located in the outskirts of Nairobi, Kenya, in East Africa.

UNEP is the heartbeat of a struggle to stem the advancing
Sahara, to alleviate the hunger of Somalia and Sudan, to focus and
diminish the earth's fears of acid rain, of ozone gaps, of greenhouse
effects, to battle for the preservation of species around the globe, to
conserve the wildlife and its habitats in Tanzania, Brazil, Zimbabwe
and elsewhere—to protect the earth from the voracious appetite of
heedless humankind.

Nairobi was an appropriate place for me to awake anew to
the urgency, immediacy and simplicity of our planet's environmental crisis.

Emotions I had first experienced in the tropical rain forests
of Latin America and sensed in the aftermath of Central American
deforestation and hurricane damage, resurfaced when I flew over
the headwaters of the Nile and personally confronted the problems
of a once-verdant Africa, now blighted with drought.

I had studied what the Bible has to say about God's purposes in creation and our responsibility as his stewards of the
earth's indispensable resources and matchless beauty. As I began to
put things together in equatorial East Africa, it impressed me that

our biggest need at this moment is simply an awareness of what the oft-mentioned "environmental crisis" is all about.

The feeling came over me—and persists to this day—that if we can manage to understand the problem, we may be able to make the right decisions, consent to the appropriate "tradeoffs," assume the proper attitudes and fulfill our human and Christian responsibilities. What we need, therefore, is a "Primer of Ecology"—a statement profound enough to affect our postures and our actions, but simple enough to avoid misunderstanding or ignorance.

Some simple ABCs of ecology

"Awareness" is the key word for us at this moment of history.

This is why I began to focus on some simple ABCs of ecology—coming up with a couple of suggested figures and formulae for describing the nature and dimensions of the earth's present and growing environmental crisis.

It starts with the concept of balance. Life is best when everything is kept in equilibrium, whether it's eating, exercise, sleep, work or recreation. Too much or too little is dangerous. We find safety on the middle ground of moderation.

When Vice President Al Gore called his recent environmental book *Earth in the Balance*[6] he made an appropriate title choice, because that is what ecology is all about—balance. Ecology deals with consumption and supply, with depletion and restoration, with refuse and recycling. It must balance resources and renewal. It is the science of life in all its relationships. For life to be sustainable, we must keep all of these in careful equilibrium.

Dr. Calvin DeWitt, in his contribution to the book *Growing Our Future*, has described succinctly how life is sustained in the earth's biosphere.

"The world works as a symphony of material and life cycles," he says, "all powered by Earth's star, the sun, in which solar heating drives the global circulations of water and air in patterns shaped by unequal heating and topographic relief." He explains that by a process of photosynthesis, the solar light energizes all of life "through a mesh-work of molecule-to-molecule and organism-to-organism energy transfers."[7]

In these transfers, DeWitt goes on to say, the "biotic and physical components, thus empowered, interactively exchange matter and energy to form and maintain the life-sustaining biophysical fabric of the biosphere and its component ecosystems."

Paul Kennedy uses different language to describe the same phenomena:

> In thermodynamic terms the earth is a closed system, meaning that no material enters or leaves it except for the sun's radiant energy, and the only processes that can occur are those in which material is changed from one form to another . . .
>
> If this closed system is to run indefinitely, therefore, the transformation process must ultimately constitute a closed cycle, in which material returns to its original form: new resource becomes useful matter which becomes waste which is then absorbed back into the ecosystem to become future raw material. When functioning properly, it is a beautiful and wonderful self-sustaining cycle of life.[8]

The earth's biosphere as gyroscope

If this still sounds complicated to you, let me suggest that you look at the earth's biosphere as if it were a gyroscope. A gyroscope maintains a perfect equilibrium by allowing one wheel to spin inside another. In this case, the sun provides the necessary energy to drive the earth.

If we were to try to picture this activity, it might look something like Figure 1.1 on page 12.

What you are looking at is really a simplified, healthy ecosystem, fired by the sun's energy, and moderately affected by human activity. Solar power interacts with matter in processes of consumption and renewal, releasing energy and producing waste.

Figure 1.1 - How the world works

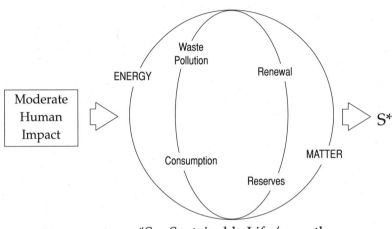

ENERGY

Waste
Pollution

Renewal

Moderate
Human
Impact

S*

Consumption

MATTER

Reserves

*S = Sustainable Life/growth

In turn, some other ecosytem recycles the waste, releasing energy and "storing" matter. Nature ultimately uses both in further processes. The end product is sustainable life or growth.

The earth's biosphere is such an ecosystem—or rather, a complex of many such ecosystems—which is self-sustaining and can tolerate a moderate impact of "outside" forces, such as human intervention.

Factors built into the equation correct natural imbalances. To take an overly simple example: If things get out of balance and gardens are being destroyed by a plague of too many rabbits, nature ultimately can reduce this threat by bringing in foxes and other predators that include rabbits in their food chain.

Sometimes, disease and starvation can also serve to bring an excess of one or another species back into balance. The gradual adaptation of that species to different foods and conditions can also accomplish the same thing.

Within certain limits, therefore, the earth's ecosphere is capable of dealing with damaging factors that temporarily upset its equilibrium. For example, it has survived the impact of asteroids, the deep freeze of ice ages, the scarring of many droughts, floods, plagues and pestilences. The gyroscope may wobble a bit, but it is ultimately powerful enough to recover its balance and to keep on spinning.

Excessive human impact and the environment's balance

Our basic problem today, however, is that our environment is being thrown out of balance by excessive human impact. Human assault is more dangerous than other natural forces because as human beings in God's creation we are unique.

The human race is one of many species on the earth, and subject to the natural laws to which I have referred. At the same time, as those who have been created in the "image of God," we also have the capacity to affect, modify and control many aspects of our ecosphere. The Bible calls this capability and responsibility "stewardship."

Figure 1.2 - Where we are today:
The disastrous effect of excessive human impact

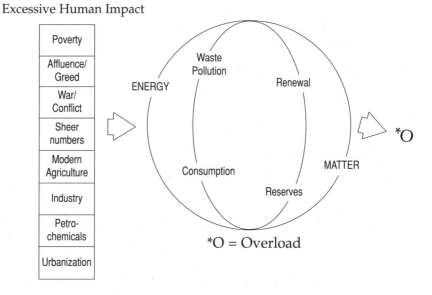

Excessive Human Impact

| Poverty |
| Affluence/ Greed |
| War/ Conflict |
| Sheer numbers |
| Modern Agriculture |
| Industry |
| Petro- chemicals |
| Urbanization |

ENERGY

Waste Pollution

Renewal

Consumption

Reserves

MATTER

*O

*O = Overload

Humankind, however, has not exercised this stewardship in earthkeeping ways, but with careless disregard for conservation and equilibrium. This planet now holds more than five billion human inhabitants. The earth's ecosystems today are under immense pressure. With such a burden can the gyroscope keep spinning?

Before it is too late, we need to assess carefully the impact of human populations on their natural environment. Figure 1.2 on page 13 shows where our abuse of nature and of natural resources has brought us in 1993—to the brink of disaster!

As we analyze the component factors of human impact on the environment, you may wonder why I have put "poverty" at the top of the list. That is because poverty is a major contributing cause to several other critical factors, such as excessive population, urbanization and social conflict, or war—all of which together produce environmental overload.

As we shall see in the next chapter, while God expects humankind to work hard he never intended for poverty to be a prevailing state of human existence. The Bible shows very clearly that God deplores poverty, expresses special love and concern for the poor and promises *shalom* and sufficiency to the faithful. Poverty is part of the curse of human sin that touches, directly or indirectly, every descendant of Adam and Eve.

Many studies have shown that excessive population growth is, to some degree, a result of poverty.[9] This is because children are a part of the productive capacity of families. If a family lacks economic security, then having more children is a reasonable choice for parents. The problem is that the overpopulation then turns around and worsens the poverty that helped to cause it.

Furthermore, if poor parents know that as many as one-third of their children may die in infancy, they may feel that they need an extra cushion as well. When there is a growing sense of economic security, however, birth rates drop.

It is the sheer number of human beings that eventually overwhelms their environmental habitat. Yet the massive elimination of people, whether by starvation, war, or whatever means, is obviously not the Christian—nor the human—response. The causes of overpopulation are what we need to bring under control.

The elite few and the poor majority

Affluence, except for the elite few, is a relatively modern phenomenon. Never in history have there been so many comfortably prosperous people in the world as today. On the other hand, never have there been so many people starving and trapped in grinding poverty.

The problem is that affluence breeds inequity, envy, greed and waste. In the centuries when hunters and gatherers composed most of the earth's population, everyone received an equal distribution of all food and game. But with the private ownership of property and the creation of armies and professional elites, common resources became bones of contention and triggers of social breakdown.

There is something obviously wrong when the world's developed countries, with about 22 percent of its population, consume some 82 percent of its commercial sources of energy, leaving only 18 percent for the remaining three-quarters of the human race.[10]

To be even more specific, the U.S., with five percent of the world's population, uses 40 percent of the world's mineral and 30 percent of its energy resources. Paradoxically, shameful numbers of homeless poor, rising rates of infant mortality and skyrocketing surges of violence and abuse plague the nation.

During his or her lifetime, each child born in the U.S. state of California will probably use 20 times the resources required for a child in Colombia or India. We need to factor this disproportion into our demographic findings about the increase of population worldwide. It may not be the increasing numbers of the world's poor, but rather the insatiable appetites of its wealthy, which will ultimately prove to be our undoing.

Even modern agriculture—although it has made possible the feeding of the earth's mushrooming population—has been ruthless in its impact on our environment. Mechanical cultivation

15

and the artificial injection of chemical fertilizers have forced mis-used soils—overworked, leached and eroded—to produce beyond their normal capacity. One result has been the massive contamination of water tables and downstream rivers, plus dustbowls, major erosion, salinization and desertification in many important parts of the globe.

Industry, of course, has been a producer of affluence and a provider of many of modern life's comforts. But it has also triggered massive migration to the cities, causing the innumerable problems of urbanization and urban ghettos. It has also been the voracious consumer of the planet's raw resources, and the producer of immense quantities of toxic chemicals and pollutants, all of which it discharges into the land, water or atmosphere.

Altogether, we have escalated the human impact on our biosphere to a stage above overload, and we stand today on the brink of disaster. "Can humanity survive?" is not a frivolous question.

2

What it would need to regain its balance

This is where we need to pause and take a deep breath!

We have just affirmed, in effect, the mortality of the earth. Humanity has skewed the balance of consumption and renewal almost beyond recognition. The gyroscope is faltering. The forces are out of control. The "good" creation of our loving God is limping painfully.

Every increase in population puts additional stress on the environment. World population did not reach one billion until A.D. 1830. It took another century—until 1930—to grow to two billion. Only 30 years later, however, it had reached three billion. Fifteen years after that, in 1975, it had increased to four billion—twice the number of persons who were alive for World War II. The population is now increasing by one billion every seven years or so. In many parts of the world there are already far too many inhabitants for the life support systems that they must depend on.[11]

The carelessness with which we are consuming our planetary resources in the current century is alarmingly obvious. Some of these resources are renewable, but many are not—at least not fast enough to delay the downward plunge towards exhaustion.

Petroleum, precious metals, firewood and even farmland are increasingly scarce. We have not developed alternative energy sources. Nuclear power plants have become time bombs. Even more sinister is the elimination of species and varieties of life forms on the planet, foreshadowing poverty and disaster. The leveling of forests is a global symptom of this catastrophe.

On a par with careless consumption is the massive production of waste, pollution and the toxic contamination of water, land and atmosphere. This results from greedy lifestyles, industrial indifference and the accumulation of by-products that are not biodegradable. Carbon dioxide—and therefore planetary temperatures—is on the increase. Protective ozone layers in the atmosphere are dissipated.

The accumulation and interaction of all these factors leave the earth in a sorry mess we can only describe as a **disaster**. Many doomsayers predict a total collapse of the earth's ecosystems, possibly in the early part of the twenty-first century.

What should Christians do?

Is there any hope for our planet? Is there a Christian understanding and a Christian solution for our human dilemma?

It is my conviction that our prime need at this time still is awareness—awareness of what the Scriptures can tell us about the past and the future of our universe, awareness of what the ecological crisis is all about, and awareness of our responsibility to know and to act in sound, earthkeeping ways—how to patch the garment we must continue to wear as long as we can.

Even more pressing, however—because it involves eternal as well as environmental interests—is to share with the earth's people everywhere the life-changing gospel of Jesus Christ. There is no more effective means of transforming human attitudes than by the regeneration of human hearts. The best way to overcome poverty, to thwart greed, to temper affluence, to reduce conflict, to increase compassion and to moderate lifestyles is to spread the Good News of Christ's love and regenerative power.

Nothing else can provide liberation from the evil in the world. The Christian ethic is the world's only hope of averting environmental disaster. This ethic also happens to coincide with our own best—even selfish—interests. Symbiotically, the stark reality of deterioration in the ecosphere of human existence reinforces the Christian ethic's importance.

As the ecological crisis becomes more acute, therefore, it is increasingly apparent that the path of survival—and probably that of economic profitability—leads directly to the protection of our environment and the careful stewardship of our resources. This convergence of Christian and survival objectives is humanity's best hope for continued life on the planet.[12]

Evangelism thus becomes an essential part of patching God's garment. Ecology is not just for Christians, but Christian principles are of prime importance in finding a solution to our crisis.

A brief review of the science of ecology

If this is what we must do to patch God's garment (see Figure 2.1 on page 20), let's start at the beginning.

Until the 1960s, ecology in most of the world was an esoteric science of botanists and zoologists who studied plants and animals in their habitats. Its purview was very narrow. Scholars were very focused in their research. Ecology texts did not mention humankind and its environment. The only man-made threat to the earth was the atom bomb.

At the same time as the publication of Rachel Carson's eloquent book *Silent Spring* (1962)[13]—and probably in large part because of it—came a sudden awareness of humanity's intimate involvement with the planet and its natural systems. Agricultural chemistry became a hot topic among biologists. The generational rebellion and the "greening of America" were powerful social motors.

Ecology, according to a statement by Eugene P. Odum in 1970, within the previous two years had undergone a "historic attitude revolution" and had grown to include "the totality of man and his environment."[14] By "Earth Day" in 1970, Odum said, scientists had come to realize that humanity faced ultimate planetary limitations rather than simply local shortages.

We can describe ecology (from the Greek *oikos*, meaning "home" or "habitat," hence "environment") as understanding the

Figure 2.1 - Where we need to be: Equilibrium restored

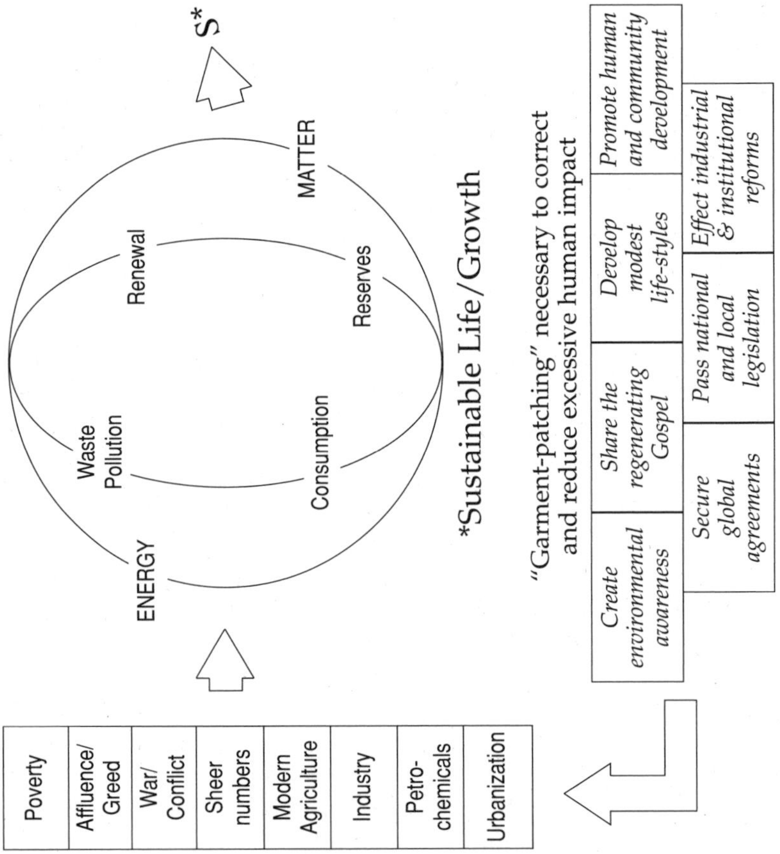

| Poverty |
| Affluence/ Greed |
| War/ Conflict |
| Sheer numbers |
| Modern Agriculture |
| Industry |
| Petro-chemicals |
| Urbanization |

ENERGY

Waste Pollution

Renewal

MATTER

Consumption

Reserves

S*

*Sustainable Life/Growth

"Garment-patching" necessary to correct and reduce excessive human impact

| Create environmental awareness | Share the regenerating Gospel | Develop modest life-styles | Promote human and community development |
| Secure global agreements | Pass national and local legislation | Effect industrial & institutional reforms | |

various forms of life in their respective contexts. That's a tall order. It seems at first to embrace all natural science. To a certain extent, it does.

But ecology becomes less formidable when you realize that it focuses narrowly on relationships, on systems of dependence and on forms of interaction. It doesn't attempt to solve the mystery of life itself, nor does it analyze each life form in detail. It merely examines the fabrics into which they are woven.

So a "garment" becomes a very apt metaphor for describing the environment, which is the context of all living species. An infinite number of delicate threads weave all the diverse patterns and textures of our ecosystem into a single garment.

A relatively simple science at first, ecology over the years has expanded with the rapid growth of knowledge. Now it embraces virtually everything, because we now know that almost everything in the universe is to some degree interdependent. Food chains and energy exchanges connect the ecosystems of microscopic life forms, insects, animals, birds, marine creatures, flora, human and other species, in one vast "bundle of life."

This makes it impossible for any of us to be full-blown ecologists. We can see only part of the picture. Biologists often seem to understand the problems best. But economists, chemists, physicists, agronomists and industrialists—all have something important to say about the relationships of ecological systems. And, of course, life and its relationships are—or should be—a central focus of theology.

Ecological awareness and personal pilgrimages

Ecological awareness is most often the product of a personal pilgrimage. Vice President Gore, for example, tells of his boyhood on a farm. On this farm he was taught to dam the gullies in the fields before the rain could turn them into deep slashes in which the torrents of water could erode the soil and reduce the farm's productivity. His awareness grew through his mother's reaction to Carson's *Silent Spring*. Eventually, his accumulated experience and knowledge made him a major spokesman in government on behalf of environmental issues and interests.[15]

Dr. Paul Brand tells how a *Handful of Mud* and a grandfather-philosopher in a rice paddy of India started his young mind on the road to environmental awareness.[16]

My own fascination with ecology surfaced when I first experienced the virgin rain forests in Costa Rica. It didn't really become in any degree obsessive, however, until our family acquired a small farm in a forested area. Because of this farm, I got involved in conserving and renewing the jungle growth to protect its beauty and resources.

Nothing can match the first-time impact of towering cedro macho trees, graceful laurels and broad-branched hardwoods, hanging vines and ubiquitous shrubs, all embracing each other while hosting parasite orchids and vegetation, their density pierced here and there by jungle palms stretching up for light.

Sometimes dark, mysterious and menacing, the rain forest can also be intermittently brilliant and glorious. Bright, flowered palmettos, abundant ferns and thickets, tangled roots with twigs, leaves, seeds and mud underfoot—the jungle is both formidable and beautiful, representing thousands of years of seemingly random, but totally interdependent, purposeful, ecological development.

Exotic parrots, toucans and quetzales spread their wings above it. Hundreds of animals—from insects to rodents to carnivores—scurry through it, most of them invisible to the untrained eye. It is an abundant cornucopia of varieties and species, a prolific slice of life—a genuine cross-section of God's amazing creation.

To tell the truth, I never had a green thumb, nor much patience—and certainly no skill—in the farming side of things. I was much more interested in cattle, loved the horseback riding it involved, and began to acquire some understanding of trees and ecology.

The fascination of the tropical rain forest

What most intrigued me was the tropical rain forest itself— including the 14 year-round water sources we discovered on the farm and the things we had to do to keep them flowing. I must have planted a thousand trees—everything from citrus and other fruits to giant eucalypti, from bamboo to pines—trying to develop contiguous patches of jungle and provide the variety to attract animal wildlife and feathered species.

At various times we saw a deer, a sloth, a mountain lion, monkeys, tepezquintles (a large and delicious forest rodent), and many varieties of snakes and birds. Once I had to step around an eleven-foot boa that was asleep on the trail leading to the farm. On two occasions one of our huts was totally "vacuumed" by a passing horde of "white" ants that ate every bit of organic garbage—such as dead insects—in their path. Walls, ceilings, floor cracks— nature's cleaning crew left everything immaculate.

You are quickly overwhelmed by how fast things grow in rain forest country—fence posts break out in foliage, pastures bounce back from being leveled by cattle, saplings become trees in almost no time at all. Life and verdure are all around you.

Most of this abundant life seems to focus in the trees. They provide the healing shade, the sure refuge, the tasty leaves, healthy fruits and nourishing nuts. They anchor the soil and loosen the earth, preventing erosion and aiding irrigation. They turn carbon dioxide into oxygen, and nitrogen into proteins. They diffuse the wind and ultimately sacrifice their lumber for the necessities of humanity and beast.

No wonder it begins to hurt when you see these pillars of the rain forest felled and burned to provide more space for pasture or agriculture—space that people often abandon to erosion or desertification once quick crops exhaust its immediate nutrients.

The soil of the forest is thin—70 percent of its biological wealth is above the ground in the life and moisture of the trees. Their shady canopy protects the soil from the sun's damaging rays and passes water back to the rain clouds to be dropped elsewhere. The soil itself is highly vulnerable when exposed to the elements.

Gradually, I came to understand the perils of the slash-and-burn destruction of natural forests, the constant tension of food today versus resources tomorrow, the disappearance of species and the barrenness of overworking the land.

Loss of trees and tropical rain forests is not the only problem our dying planet faces. Other problems are just as pressing, and we shall mention them in subsequent chapters. But this is where I come from. My environmental pilgrimage took me through the rain forest.

Humanity and the environment together form God's creation

For me, it was a fundamentally religious experience. Therefore, in this book I shall refer to humanity and its environment together as God's creation, with thanks to Calvin DeWitt for his initiative in this regard.[17] To speak of God's handiwork as "nature and humanity" is to foster a misleading dichotomy.

Humankind is indeed different from the rest of the natural world, because God made us in his image and breathed his spirit into us. But we are just as definitely an integral part of the earth's biosphere and participants in several of its ecosystems. So I choose to discourage dichotomy and to use DeWitt's preferred term, "creation."

I am not an ecologist—not even a trained naturalist. But I believe that from a lifetime of experience and from the Bible, I received a framework of knowledge into which I can fit the facts as they become known to me. I propose to share these facts and this framework in the pages that follow.

I invite you to join me on the path of discovery that leads to environmental awareness.

3
The way the Bible tells it

The cornerstone of Christian ecology is stewardship.

Human beings are the only creatures on earth who possess to any degree the capability of controlling and managing the environment. Christians believe that this is innate in the divine image stamped on all humans—not just on believing Christians—by God in creation.

Christians also believe that divine mandate entrusted stewardship of the environment specifically to the human race. The Bible affirms it.

> . . . you have made him [humankind] only a little lower than the angels, and placed a crown of glory and honor upon his head. You have put him in charge of everything you made; everything is put under his authority. (Ps. 8:5-6)

Admittedly, the early chapters of Genesis—where this is explained—are full of poetry and imagery. But clearly God created humankind in his own image and conferred on us the responsibility of earthkeeping.

It is also interesting to learn that Christianity is not the only religion to recognize human stewardship of the created world. It seems to be a part of the so-called "cultural mandate" that is bred into humankind. Islam, Buddhism and, of course, the Jewish faith make similar affirmations.

By inference, it is equally clear that we have failed to live up to God's requirements and that the devastation of the environment has come back to haunt us.

God tells Adam and Eve about the Creation

The Lord God apparently derived great pleasure from the world he had made, and we learn from Genesis 3:8 that he walked in the Garden of Eden and conversed with Adam, the crown of his creation. Genesis does not clearly specify whether God came in visible form—a "theophany," as when he appeared to Abraham, for example—or whether he made himself known by an audible voice, as at the baptism and the transfiguration of Jesus.

Using the language and imagery of Scripture, however, we can eavesdrop on one of these conversations, which may have sounded something like this:[18]

"Tell me, Lord God, how you made the world."

Adam sat on a grassy spot under the intensely green shade of a spreading mango tree. He focused his eyes not on the splendor of the tropical tree garden around him, but on the spot where he imagined the Voice to be. It was one of his frequent afternoon conversations with the Lord God, his Creator and friend. Eve, his God-given bride, was resting beside him.

"I've told you the story several times," the Voice responded. "Why do you want to hear it again?"

"Because it's a beautiful story," Adam answered, "and besides, I want Eve to hear it directly from you."

After a pause, the Voice spoke again:

"Eve, do you, like Adam, want to hear the story?"

"Yes, my Lord God."

"Then let me tell it to you this time in poetic terms and symbols. When I began the process of creating the earth and the heavens, everything at first was a shapeless, almost chaotic mass, and my Spirit hovered over the dark vapors like a mother hen.

"So I said, *'Let there be light.' And light appeared* (Gen. 1:3). This pleased me and I separated the light from the darkness, letting it shine for a while, and then letting the darkness creep in again.

The light time I called 'day' and the dark time I called 'night.' Together they marked the first day of creation.

"The next day, I separated the vapors, using their gases to form the atmosphere and the skies above and their liquids to make the waters below. This took place on the second day.

"Then by my command, the waters under the sky were gathered into oceans, so that the dry land could emerge, pushing up into mountains, plains, valleys and coastlines. I called the dry land 'earth' and the waters 'seas.'

"The whole effect was very pleasing to me, so I called for the land to burst forth with every sort of grass and seed-bearing plant. Fruit trees sprang up with seeds inside their fruit. This was so that the seeds would produce the kinds of plants and fruits they came from. All of this happened on the third day, and I was delighted."

Adam's eyes brightened, and Eve sat up a little straighter. "Do you mean that each tree can reproduce itself?" she asked.

"Yes," the Voice replied, "and more than that. The trees also convert energy from the skies into life for the other parts of creation. You see, on the fourth day I called for bright lights in the sky to give light and energy to the earth and to distinguish the day and the night, and to establish the seasons of the earth and to mark the passage of the days and years.

"I made two immense lights to shine on the earth—the larger one, the sun, bursting with energy, to rule over the day and the smaller one, the moon, to preside through the night, along with innumerable stars. I set them in the sky to light the earth and to divide the light from the darkness. The result was pleasing. This was what took place on the fourth day.

"Then I said, *'Let the waters teem with fish and other life, and let the skies be filled with birds of every kind'* (Gen. 1:20). So I created huge sea mammals, and every kind of fish and every sort of bird. *And [I] looked at them with pleasure, and blessed them all. 'Multiply and stock the oceans,' [I] told them. And to the birds [I] said, 'Let your numbers increase. Fill the earth!' That ended the fifth day* (Gen. 1:22, 23).

"I then called upon the earth to bring forth every kind of animal—cattle for domestication and reptiles and wildlife of every kind. And so it came to pass, and I was very pleased with what I had done."

God creates man and woman

The Voice paused pensively, then continued.

"It was a beautiful world, and it pleased me. Yet it lacked something. It was as if I had built a charming dwelling place without being able to live in it, or a lovely garden that I could only enjoy from a distance. I wanted to be a part of it.

"So I said, *'Let us make a man—someone like ourselves, to be the master of all life upon the earth and in the skies and in the seas'* (Gen. 1:26).

"Then I formed your body, Adam, from the dust of the ground, like all the other mammals, but I breathed into that body the divine breath of life. And you became a living person—at one with the earth but formed in the image of God. Through you, and through the woman I have taken from your side, I can enjoy with full pleasure this beautiful world that we share.

"Man and woman I created you, so that you could love each other, and like the rest of creation, have offspring and replenish the earth and care for it on my behalf. You are masters of the fish and birds and all the animals. They will all be known by the names you give them.

"You are also my custodians of creation's beauty, its integrity and its truth. These are the qualities with which you will enhance your own life together. Be fruitful, therefore, and populate the earth for me.

"*And look! I have given you the seed-bearing plants throughout the earth, and all the fruit trees for your food. And I've given all the grass and plants to the animals and birds for their food* (Gen. 1:29-30).

"In truth, I saw now that the world was excellent in every way. This was how the sixth day ended, and on the seventh day I rested."

Adam was familiar with the rest of the story, but Eve hung eagerly on the words the Voice was saying to them, and both of them sensed something of the awe and significance of the Lord God's statement.

"Then," the Voice went on, "I planted a garden in Eden, towards the east, and placed both of you in it. I put all sorts of beautiful trees here, *trees producing the choicest of fruit. At the center of the garden [I] placed the Tree of Life, and also the Tree of Conscience, giving knowledge of Good and Bad* (Gen. 2:9). A river flows through this Garden of Eden to water it.

"I have placed you, Adam, and you, Eve, in this beautiful arboretum as its gardeners to tend and care for it. You and your descendants are the stewards of my creation. It is mine, but I put it in your hands. Love it, use it, keep it and care for it and it will serve you well.

"And that, Adam, is the story you asked for. May it live comfortably in your heart and memory."

The intrusion of sin

The intrusion of sin into such an idyllic setting was incredibly devastating. It must have broken God's heart, and it condemned his human creatures to endless misery.

The Lord God did not create Adam and Eve to play puppets. He wanted companions—human, to be sure, and not divine—but beings to whom he could reveal himself, with whom he could share his pleasures and who could find in him their own security and fulfillment.

For this to happen, the earthlings needed to seek his friendship of their own free volition—and not respond in a merely mechanical way, at the end of a puppet string. So the Lord God gave them a simple test and allowed them to be "on their own." In a world full of opportunities and enjoyment, there was only one prohibition: they were to abstain from eating the fruit of the tree in the center of the Garden of Eden, "the tree of the knowledge of good and evil" (Gen. 2:16, NIV). This was to be the trial of their loyalty and obedience.

Many Christians believe this story is literally true. But whether it is history for many Christians or parable for unbelievers, the fact remains that humanity failed the test. Instead of heeding the voice of God, Adam and Eve chose to follow the advice of the serpent in an ego trip of conscious disobedience. The result was disastrous, and it affected their relationship with their friend and Creator.

That evening they heard the sound of the Lord God walking in the garden, and they hid among the trees.

"What are you hiding from?" the Voice called out.

"I heard your footsteps and knew you were coming," Adam replied, "and I didn't want you to see me naked. So I hid."

"Who told you that you were naked?" the Lord God asked. "Did you eat the fruit of that tree I warned you about" (Gen. 3:11)?

"Yes," Adam admitted, "but it was given to me by the woman you gave me to be my wife. She brought me some, and I ate it."

"How could you do such a thing?" the Lord God asked the woman.

"It was the serpent who tricked me," she replied.

The Lord God turned to the serpent. *"This is your punishment,"* he said. *"You are singled out from among all the domestic and wild animals of the whole earth—to be cursed.*

"You shall grovel in the dust as long as you live, crawling along on your belly. From now on you and the woman will be enemies, as will all of your offspring and hers. And I will put the fear of you into the woman, and between your offspring and hers. He shall strike you on your head, while you will strike at his heel" (Gen. 3:14-15).

The Voice then focused on the woman.

"You shall bear children in intense pain and suffering," he told Eve. *"Yet even so, you shall welcome your husband's affections, and he shall be your master"* (Gen. 3:16).

"As for you, Adam," the Lord God said, *"because you listened to your wife and ate the fruit when I told you not to, I have placed a curse upon the soil. All your life you will struggle to extract a living from it. It will grow thorns and thistles for you, and you shall eat its grasses.*

"All your life you will sweat to master it, until your dying day. Then you will return to the ground from which you came. For you were made from the ground, and to the ground you will return" (Gen. 3:17-19).

Instead of being humanity's friend and servant, as God had first intended, sin transformed nature into Adam's enemy, to be subdued and forced into production as though by slavery. God did not revoke the exercise of human stewardship over the created world. Our stewardship simply became much more difficult and less enjoyable.

No longer were Adam and Eve at ease in their garden paradise. God barred them from Eden and forced them to live in hostile territory, defending themselves from the elements and wild animals and struggling to make the earth productive to meet their need for food and sustenance.

Humankind's stewardship continued after the Flood

That God did not revoke the stewardship, however, became very evident in the story of Noah and the Flood.

The rampant evil that erupted in the generations succeeding Adam and Eve pained the Lord God's heart. First, Cain murdered his brother Abel. Later there were many who lusted after the *"beautiful earth women and took any they desired to be their wives"* (Gen. 6:1).

Meanwhile, the crime rate was rising rapidly across the earth, and, as seen by God, the world was rotten to the core (Gen. 6:11). The condition of humankind made God "sorry he had made them" (Gen. 6:6). *"I will blot out from the face of the earth all mankind that I created,"* he said. *"Yes, and the animals too, and the reptiles and the birds. For I am sorry I made them"* (Gen. 6:7).

Only Noah brought pleasure to the Lord God. He was righteous and faithful. God charged Noah with the construction of a large boat equipped to carry his family and pairs (i.e., male and female) of specimens from every wild and domesticated species of the creatures of land and air. (Of the animals and birds God had chosen for eating and for sacrifices, Noah was to save seven pairs.) In this ark the Lord God preserved a cross section of his created life through 150 days of massive flood.

The story (Gen. 6, 7, 8 and 9) is a beautiful example of God's concern for every living thing. Once Noah and his passengers had safely survived the Flood, God placed a rainbow as a sign in the sky. This was a sign not just to Noah's family, but "to you and to all the earth," promising that God would never repeat such a whole-sale destruction. To Noah he renewed his charge of stewardship.

Are Christians to blame for the current crisis?

Some modern ecologists have tried to blame our current environmental crisis on what they call a long-time prevalence of allegedly "Christian" attitudes of antagonism towards nature and the earth's ecosystems. They have, however, misunderstood humanity's stewardship within the created world, thinking that God intended it as a license to conquer and exploit rather than an obligation to care for, protect and develop.

If one looks at the history of our so-called Christian era, their accusation is not an unreasonable one. Yet it comes from con-fusing "Christianity" with the culture that has grown around it— better described as "Christendom."

While Christendom has often helped to devastate and exhaust our natural environment, this attitude of greed and exploitation is not Christian. Instead, it is anti-Christian—the antithesis of Christian stewardship. For the genuine Christian, humankind's responsibility for conserving and repairing the earth's ecosystems still stands.

Of course, we must recognize that for centuries, because of the abundance of nature's resources, Christians and non-Christians alike have done little to conserve and renew them. This is a tragedy—a collective crime—but it does not manifest a Christian attitude. And now, at this point of our experience, our failure through the years simply reinforces our obligation to do whatever we can to rectify our sinful neglect in the past.

Another problem for Christians is that for many centuries we were taught to think of sin primarily in terms of subjective atti-tudes, like unbelief and rejection. That in itself is not wrong. Indeed, it is extremely important.

Yet by focusing on the internal and the personal, we have tended to overlook the social and environmental dimensions of our disobedience—the effect of sin on the human community, and its impact on the ecological "envelope" into which the Lord God has inserted us for survival, the "garment" with which he has clothed us, to use the language of Psalm 102.

Sin begins at the seat of the human will. It poisons the heart and spreads corrosively throughout the body, touching every level of existence, including our society and our environment. "What is causing the quarrels and fights among you?" James asks. "Isn't it because there is a whole army of evil desires within you?" (James 4:1). Sin is the cause of war, moral decay, social corruption, environmental degradation and natural disasters.

The environment shares in humankind's sin and redemption

It is not difficult for us to appreciate how our sinfulness can affect the society of which we are members. It does not occur to us quite so readily, however, that our sin has also contaminated the environment. But we are just as much a part of our biosphere as we are a part of human society, our "sociosphere." Human sin, therefore, is just as much the root cause of famine as it is of war—of natural disasters as it is of social sickness.

There is a more positive, flip side to this truth. If the environment and its ecosystems—along with society and its institutions—are linked inextricably with the human race, and suffer with us the consequences of human sin and condemnation, then they also share in humankind's redemption and renewal.

This thought is alien to most of our traditional theological beliefs. The narrow individualism of our Christianity too often leads us astray. The Shorter or Longer Catechisms do not reflect environmental concerns. Christian creeds in general are strictly personalized.

According to the Apostles' Creed—regularly used in many churches—the end product of salvation is simply "the forgiveness of sin, the resurrection of the body and life everlasting." Traditionally, apart from vague and passing references to a "new heaven and a new earth," our common body of Christian doctrine has not embraced the environment.

This is evidence that as earthlings we have not heard what God has said, neither have we understood our own intrinsic relationship to the rest of creation—to the ecosystems of which we are a part. Nor have we attempted systematically to apply our salvation in Christ to the environment.

When God sent his Son into the world to bear vicariously the punishment of evil in the human race, he provided the basis of forgiveness for people. But he also provided the promise of a renewed society and a renewed environment—the kingdom of God and the new heavens and the new earth.

This seems to be the clear message of Romans chapter eight and the clear grounds for Christian hope in this age of social and environmental decay.

If stewardship is the foundation of Christian ecology, and death the price of disobedience, then hope and resurrection must become its fulfillment. Then God's much-patched garment will be replaced for eternity.

4

Disasters are natural

"Master," his disciples asked him [Jesus], "why was this man born blind? Was it a result of his own sins or those of his parents?" (John 9:2)

They had met the blind man on the streets of Jerusalem. We do not know whether the disciples were moved by compassion or by curiosity. But they raised a question most people have asked themselves at one time or another.

The inheritance of original sin

If evil has come into the world through sin, and if the sinful behavior of its victims sometimes worsens it, how can we know who is at fault? The question Jesus's disciples asked was not an idle one.

His reply, however, made it clear that the general curse of sin and the wages of one's own sins are two different things. While it may be true that sometimes we are punished for wrong actions, there are also many wrongs, injustices and hardships in the human experience for which no one in particular is to blame. They are a part of the inheritance of "original sin."

"Neither this man nor his parents sinned," Jesus answered his disciples, "but this happened so that the work of God might be displayed in his life" (John 9:3, NIV). And he healed him.

Pain, suffering, inequity—deserved more in some cases than in others—all are common to our fallen nature. Yet as Christians, God does not expect us simply to endure them in resignation—instead, they challenge us to see them as opportunities for God to show his power, grace and glory.

Jesus applied this insight to the rebels who were slaughtered in the court of the temple, and to the unfortunate victims of the Tower of Siloam when it fell. They were no more guilty of wrongdoing than were their peers in the city of Jerusalem. But their misfortune was a reminder to others of death's proximity and a challenge to courage in adversity to their survivors.

He also applied the same insight to manmade and natural environmental disasters. In Mark 13, for example, he predicted that "nations and kingdoms will proclaim war against each other, and there will be earthquakes in many lands, and famines. These herald only the early stages of the anguish ahead. But . . . this is your opportunity to tell them the Good News."

The Apostle Paul, writing to the Christians in Rome, made the point with undeniable clarity: ". . . in all things God works for the good of those who love him, who have been called according to his purpose" (Rom. 8:28, NIV).

Linking natural disasters to environmental damage

The fifty-foot tidal wave that washed so devastatingly over the Pacific coast of Nicaragua in 1992 was obviously not "anthropogenic" (i.e., of direct human origin). An earthquake beneath the ocean, 75 miles from the shore, created it. Human damage to the environment did not cause or exacerbate it. It was truly a "natural" disaster.

And yet, in almost every case—whether we are talking about earthquakes, hurricanes, volcano eruptions, tidal surges, tornadoes, cyclones, monsoons, fires or floods—there are links with environmental damage. They may affect the causes or the results, but every disaster has its environmental damage factors.

We can see this in the case of Hurricane Andrew in southern Florida, a relatively prosperous residential area. The origin and direction of the tropical storm itself were factors beyond human control. Human negligence, unsafe construction, imprudent concentrations of population, or other factors undoubtedly magnified its effects.

An even better example is Hurricane Fifi in Honduras some years ago. It became mortally destructive only after the wind and rain transformed into mudslides and floods, annihilating farms and villages and taking many lives. This was because the mountains over which the hurricane passed were deforested and the farmers had heavily planted the land in short-rooted sugar cane. This set the scene for massive erosion and destruction. Fifi's victims could not resist the tide of mud and water. Houses could not stand against it. Children could not struggle to the surface. Fifi was an environmental disaster in which human error was a major cause of fatalities.

Many natural and ecological catastrophes are interrelated. Typically, a volcanic eruption in the Philippines can cause a cloud of ash that casts a shadow over a belt of ocean. This results in temperature changes that stir up the "El Niño effect" and sends hurricanes rampaging up the Pacific coast of Mexico. These disasters exist and will continue—probably getting worse as the population becomes increasingly dense and the ecosystems increasingly fragile—until the end of the world.

I should add that some scientists are suggesting that an increase in the frequency and severity of hurricanes may also be the result of global warming—the so-called "greenhouse effect" attributed to a buildup of industrial gases that traps heat and slowly warms up the planet. In the hurricane season of 1992, the storms were fewer and later, but deadlier. In August, Hurricane Andrew slammed across Florida and buried itself in Louisiana. Five days later, Typhoon Omar smashed Guam. And within two weeks, Hurricane Iniki demolished the Hawaiian island of Kauai.

The Third World and natural disasters

Natural disasters are the pangs and throes of a distressed planet. "For we know," says the apostle Paul, "that even the things of nature, like animals and plants, suffer in sickness and death as they await this great event" [i.e., "that future day when God will resurrect his children" (Rom. 8:22, 19)].

"The four horsemen of the Apocalypse ride preferentially in the skies of the Third World," says sociologist Paul Harrison.[19] This area is a tropical belt comprised of the midsection of the earth between 30 degrees north and 30 degrees south of the equator. It seems that disaster targets the tropics. This part of the world is the scene of most of the environmental destruction wrought by droughts, floods, cyclones and earthquakes—the major agents of death and devastation.

Some of the reasons for this are quite obvious. Harrison points to the "cruel sun" as the principal one. The earth needs to maintain a radiation balance, receiving and reflecting equal amounts of energy from the sun, lest it becomes overheated or excessively cold.

Because it is shaped like a ball, the earth receives the greatest concentration of the sun's rays at the equator. Our planet's global weather machine then assumes the distribution of the surplus heat to the temperate zones, using the winds, rain and ocean currents for this purpose. This helps to keep the temperature extremes within tolerably moderate levels to support human life.

As might be expected, the typical ecological formation of the humid tropics is the rain forest—what Harrison calls "a vibrant explosion of life forms." The incubator effect on biological activity also produces flourishing insect and animal life.

With the weather, however, either too much rain or too little of it plagues the tropics. When it comes, rain is erosively heavy, and fertility is reduced to valleys and deltas or to volcanically renewed areas.

In any case, when a typhoon hits Calcutta or Bangladesh, when a flood ravages the vast farmlands of China, when drought bleaches the deserts of Africa, human deforestation, industrial contamination, poor crop management and failure to prevent erosion always exacerbate the consequences.

Natural disasters and sinful acts

Other disasters are even more obviously the results of harmful or sinful acts—such as oil spills at sea, toxic waste seeping into water sources, Chernobyl-like nuclear accidents, excessive fishing, shortsighted lumbering, and bad farming techniques. So when it comes to the ecological components of disaster it is sometimes not too difficult to place blame on either an industry, its executive officers, a government or its deficient regulations.

Natural disasters are the result of sin—the sinfulness of humankind and the curse on the earth. They are not usually the fault of any specific individual or individuals. But as the years pass and populations mushroom, ecosystems are damaged and become more fragile—the earth becomes more vulnerable.

As Jesus warned us, we can expect more and greater catastrophes as the end draws near. He told his disciples:

> *And when you hear of wars and insurrections beginning, don't panic. . . . True, wars must come . . . for nation shall rise against nation and kingdom against kingdom, and there will be great earthquakes, and famines in many lands, and epidemics, and terrifying things happening in the heavens . . . when all these things begin to happen, stand straight and look up! For your salvation is near. (Luke 21:9-28)*

5

Focusing on the future

"Why are Christians so totally inconsistent!" Roy Perkins stood up indignantly.

"You guys are completely pessimistic about what human beings can do, but at the same time you naively believe that God is going to turn everything around and make it come out right in the end!" He sighed, stretched and sat down again with a hopeless gesture.

Roy was one of a group of eight university students who met under the sponsorship of the Campus Christian Center to study the Bible and pray together. As a premed student, he liked to think of himself as a budding scientist. His parents had raised him as a Christian, but the simple faith of his classmates sometimes really baffled him.

Is the Christian position inconsistent?

The group's discussion centered on the futility of trying to restore the environment of Planet Earth to adequate levels for sustaining life—a subject of profound preoccupation to their generation.

"Are you trying to say that since God has things under control we don't have to do anything to prevent the complete collapse of the earth's ecosystem?" Roy asked.

"No, not at all." It was Orrin Carlson who answered for the group. Orrin was a track star, the fastest cross-country runner in the state, and had been a confessing Christian for most of his life. He found no inconsistency in the Christian position.

"Sure, we're pessimistic about humankind and about our attempts to salvage the environment because everybody in this world is tainted by sin. To save the environment, we would have to act righteously and obey God—and that doesn't come naturally to us.

"To correct the damage that we have already done to the earth," he went on, "every human being would have to swallow his pride, eliminate his greed and live in a totally modest, unselfish, non-consumptive way. That kind of a turnaround doesn't look very probable to me. That's why I'm pessimistic."

"But at the same time," Ruth Ann Mowry chimed in, "it's not inconsistent to believe that the Lord God who made the world, and who promised to redeem it and renew it someday, will step in and create 'a new heaven and a new earth' like he tells us in the Bible, in the book of Revelation."

"That's right," Orrin concurred. "And I definitely don't agree that our optimistic expectations about God's new heaven and earth should keep us from sweating it out with our fellow human beings. We've got to do what we can to save the globe from disaster, even if we're pessimistic about what we can accomplish."

If the planet's going to die anyway, why not just leave it alone?

Roy was not satisfied. "It seems to me," he countered, perhaps with tongue in cheek, "that if the planet is going to go to pot anyway, that we ought to leave it alone and pray for God to hurry up and bring about his new heaven and new earth. Won't sound environmentalism simply delay the process?"

"You want to be a doctor, Roy," Ruth Ann shot back at him. "What kind of physician would you be if you didn't treat a sick person just because you know that he is eventually going to die? God made us stewards of the earth and we have to keep working at it as long as it hangs together, don't we?"

Ever since they first met several months earlier, Roy had admired Ruth Ann Mowry. She was pretty, to begin with, but what he liked most about her was that she seemed to "have it all together." Her friendliness and Christian character blended into each other, and she matched her sincere faith in Christ with an intellectual assurance that made Roy envious. He somehow felt it was important that she understand his position.

"I guess your analogy about my medical practice makes sense," he admitted. "But it still seems terribly pessimistic to me."

"Are you saying that it's pessimistic to believe the earth's ecosystem is eventually going to die, but that to believe in the eventual death of each human being is not?"

"I guess so, although I hadn't thought of it that way."

"That's probably because you believe in life after death for people," Ruth Ann told him. "But you haven't thought about a resurrection of the planet—or the new heavens and earth."

"Most people have never really linked sin and the fall of the human race with the state of the environment, Roy." Orrin Carlson got back into the conversation.

"Are you trying to tell me that Adam's sin was the cause of our environmental deterioration today?" Roy asked.

"Precisely," was Orrin's reply. "The fact is that we humans have impacted the whole world by our sinfulness. When Adam and Eve sinned, God placed a curse on their environment. Everything that goes wrong in nature and in the global ecosystem is directly or indirectly a result of our human greed, arrogance, carelessness and disobedience. Or else it's a part of our punishment for sin.

"When God in Christ gives us new life and establishes his church—his kingdom—he also promises to renew the heavens and earth of his original creation. That's the process we're talking about."

Looking at the Flood of Noah's time

"Could I say something?"

Eric Donaldson was one of the quieter members of the group. The son of a Southern Baptist pastor, he had been exposed to the Bible since early childhood, and when he spoke up—which was not often—he usually had something worthwhile to say. The conversation stopped while the group listened to him.

"Maybe," he ventured, "it would help us to look at the great Flood of Noah's time. That was God's way of punishing the human race for its sinfulness. Psalm 29 says that 'at the Flood, the Lord showed his control of all creation' (Ps. 29:10). But the Flood not only destroyed all the people on earth—everyone, that is, except the family of Noah, who was God's righteous friend—it also wiped out most of the animal life.

"It was an ecological calamity," he explained, "affecting all the created world, or nature. Afterwards, when God renewed his covenant with humankind, he specifically told Noah that the promise was for 'you and your children and the animals you brought with you—all these birds and cattle and wild animals.'

"According to the way I read the Scriptures," Eric continued, "the Flood was an event that anticipated the final judgment of God and his eternal covenant with the human race. I think it was the apostle Peter who referred to the coming day of judgment 'as in the days of Noah.' The Flood shows that the human race and nature are inseparably linked in God's plans."

Nature shares in humanity's hope for resurrection and salvation

Roy's eyes lit up.

"So nature is subject to sin and condemnation just like people are, and can look forward, like us, to renewal and eternal life? Is that what you're trying to tell me?" he was beginning, at least, to understand their point of view.

"No," Eric replied. "I wouldn't go so far as to say that nature sinned and God condemned it. But I believe that humanity is an integral part of our created biosphere and because of our stewardship we are something like the head on the body. When humankind sins, the rest of the biosphere has to share in the consequences of that sin, just like the body shares in the decisions the head makes."

"Exactly," Ruth Ann replied. "Nature, like humanity, is waiting for its own resurrection and salvation."

"Does the Bible say that anywhere?" Roy asked her.

"I'm not sure that it says it all in any one place," she responded, as she began flipping through her Bible, "but listen to this passage in Second Peter, chapter three:

> *The day of the Lord is surely coming, as unexpectedly as a thief, and then the heavens will pass away with a terrible noise and the heavenly bodies will disappear in fire, and the earth and everything on it will be burned up . . . But we are looking forward to God's promise of new heavens and a new earth afterwards, where there will be only goodness. (2 Pet. 3: 10, 13)*

"That's pretty definite," Roy admitted. "Is there more?"

"Yes," Ruth Ann replied, "there's a rather clear statement in Romans 8. The apostle Paul is talking about our adoption by faith into God's family, where we are his children and will share his treasures and glory. But we shall inherit them only after having shared in Christ's suffering—which I suppose means sickness and death. Although what we suffer now, Paul says, is nothing compared to the glory he will give us later.

"Now listen to this," she added with emphasis:

> *. . . all creation is waiting patiently and hopefully for that future day when God will resurrect his children. For on that day thorns and thistles, sin, death, and decay—the things that overcame the world against its will at God's command—will disappear, and the world around us will share in the glorious freedom from sin which God's children enjoy.*
>
> *For we know that even the things of nature, like animals and plants, suffer in sickness and death as they await this great event. And even we Christians, although we have the Holy Spirit within us as a foretaste of future glory, also groan to be released from pain and suffering. We, too, wait anxiously for that day when God will give us our full rights as his children, including the new bodies he has promised us—bodies that will never be sick again and will never die. (Rom. 8:19-23)*

God's plans are for all creation, not just for humankind

"Wow!" was Roy's reaction. "I never saw it that way before. God's plan of salvation is not just for people—it embraces the whole world! Is that what it means when it says 'For God so loved the world'?"

"I really think so," Orrin spoke again, "because I am told that the Greek word used in the original of this text is *cosmos*, which means the universe, or all creation. And I don't think we ought to get discouraged when we can't completely reverse the process of environmental deterioration, any more than we should give up evangelizing when we realize we can't persuade every single human being to accept Christ's gospel. But we have to try."

"Here's another passage, Roy." Ruth Ann had continued to thumb through her New Testament. "This is what we can look forward to by faith, based on God's promises." She began reading from the last chapters of Revelation:

> Then I saw a new earth . . . and a new sky, for the present earth and sky had disappeared. And I, John, saw the Holy City, the new Jerusalem, coming down from God out of heaven. It was a glorious sight, beautiful as a bride at her wedding.
>
> I heard a loud shout from the throne saying, "Look the home of God is now among men, and he will live with them and they will be his people; yes, God himself will be among them. He will wipe away all tears from their eyes, and there shall be no more death, nor sorrow, nor crying, nor pain. All of that has gone forever."
>
> And the one sitting on the throne said, "See, I am making all things new!" . . .
>
> The city itself was pure, transparent gold like glass! The wall was made of jasper, and was built on twelve layers of foundation stones inlaid with gems . . .
>
> No temple could be seen in the city, for the Lord God Almighty and the Lamb are worshiped in it everywhere. And the city has no need of sun or moon to light it, for the glory of God and of the Lamb illuminate it . . . And the glory and honor of all the

*nations shall be brought into it. Nothing evil will be permitted
in it—no one immoral or dishonest—but only those whose
names are written in the Lamb's Book of Life. (Rev. 21:1-5, 18-
19, 22-23, 26-27)*

Ruth Ann quietly closed her Bible and looked at the premed
student.

"I hope, Roy, that you can find grounds for faith in these
passages. It's important that we trust Christ for our own salvation,
of course. And I'm sure you've done that. But it's also important
that we trust him as the sovereign Lord of creation who holds the
universe in his hand. We are all bound together in the bundle of life
and only a strong faith in Christ's lordship can carry us through."

The human story is bracketed by mystery

Roy was pensive for a moment. "Nevertheless, it seems to
me," he said slowly, "that the Revelation picture of the last days is
highly imaginative. I wonder if we are meant to build any theology
on such a mystical foundation."

"You may think the book of Revelation gives a mysterious
sort of closure to human history," was Ruth Ann's response, "but
that is also the way the story began. Just because the creation was
wrapped in metaphors, it was no less real. It really happened!
We're here to demonstrate that!"

The whole group was silent for a moment. Then it was Ruth
Ann who again spoke up.

"If God spelled it out for us in scientific terms we probably
couldn't understand him anyway. The creation and renewal of such
a vast and awesome universe would be too much for our finite
minds to grasp. So it seems natural to me that the human story
should be bracketed in mystery."

"Incredible!" Even Roy was awed. His voice was almost a
whisper as he spoke deliberately to the group. "So the biblical history of the planet and of the race of earthlings for whom it is home,
ends as it began, in imagery and poetry." He almost got carried
away by the grandeur of his own statement.

"Exactly!" Orrin and Ruth Ann exclaimed in unison. And Orrin continued:

"And as human beings, our salvation by faith in Jesus Christ is paralleled by the redemption—the death and resurrection—of God's beautiful universe.

"We will live our everlasting life with our Lord in a new heaven and a new earth. This we claim by faith."

6

A Christian environmentalist's creed

I BELIEVE that:

1. In the beginning, God created the universe for his own glory and enjoyment. His crowning creation was human-kind, formed in his image from the dust of the earth, and in-breathed by God's own Spirit.

2. Man and woman were created male and female to popu-late the earth and to share with their Creator in the enjoy-ment of the beauty and productivity of the created world of which they were an integral part, linked by their origin to the life around them.

3. In-breathed by God's Spirit, man and woman jointly reflected the unity of the Godhead and represented him by exercising his stewardship over the rest of creation. God made them keepers of the garden—earthkeepers.

4. When man and woman yielded to temptation and dis-obeyed God, God banished them from his presence and condemned them to certain death. At the same time, God cursed the ground and evil engulfed the rest of the cre-ated world along with its caretakers.

5. From the beginning, God loved his human agents and gave them hope for a future redemption, but they

responded—through many generations—with willful unrighteousness and rejection.

6. After the wicked rebellion of the earth's populace and the devastating Flood of Noah's day, God renewed his covenant of stewardship and blessing. Yet men and women since that time have largely continued to ignore God's mandate. All creation remains under the pall of sin and death.

7. When God "so loved the world (cosmos) that he sent his only begotten Son," he included not only human sinners but all of fallen creation in his redemptive embrace.

8. During the present age—God's window of grace and opportunity for sinful humanity to repent and avail themselves of eternal salvation through faith in the mediatorial sacrifice of Jesus Christ—humankind is failing again to be faithful steward and godly earthkeeper. Thus, creation is a victim of overload and mortal decline.

9. While the born-again children of God wait in hope for Christ's return and the realization of their salvation, unbelieving human society persists in its downward spiral of disobedience and neglect, and the natural world continues to suffer and groan in expectation of its deliverance.

10. It is the church's mission today to spread throughout the world the good news of Christ's redemptive acts and to seek to establish God's kingdom in the hearts of all people, in their social structures and in the environment that is their context.

11. Jesus Christ will soon return to earth in fulfillment of his promise to complete his church, to establish his righteous kingdom and to create a "new heaven and a new earth" for the eternal enjoyment of his redeemed people.

Although the state of our environment seems to indicate that Christ's return is imminent, we recognize that God is the creator and sustainer of his "garment"—the universe—and that he holds sovereign authority over it, to prolong or end its existence according to his own plan and design.

12. Even as we wait for Christ's return or for our own physical death and resurrection to life eternal, we must continue to serve as yeast in the loaf of a deteriorating society and caretakers of an ailing environment, seeking to affirm Christian values and to exercise corrective patterns wherever we can—loving our neighbors as ourselves—until Jesus comes or calls us home.

> . . . *Well done, good and faithful servant; you have been faithful over a little, I will set you over much. (Matt. 25:23, RSV)*

PART II - STATUS

Worrisome Holes, Threadbare Spots and Hopeful Patches

7
Population and pollution

The most recent—and possibly the most significant—hinge of environmental history was the Earth Summit in Río de Janeiro, Brazil, from June 3-14, 1992. Representatives from more than 170 national governments attended this corner-turning celebration of UNEP's (United Nations Environmental Programme) twentieth birthday, and the consensus of their resolves exceeded expectations.

Although he tried to stay in the background, the Brazil Summit was a personal triumph for Maurice Strong. Strong is the Canadian businessman who so ably coordinated the first UN Conference on the Environment in Stockholm in 1972, and who directed the establishment of the UNEP headquarters in Nairobi, Kenya.

"The level of awareness created by this conference has been immense," UN development officers reported after the Brazil gathering.[20]

To most environmentalists, this is good news indeed.

Environmentalism: A common cause among the world's nations

As we can see in his "Global Marshall Plan" (see chapter 10), U.S. Vice President Al Gore advocates environmentalism as a new and common cause among the world's nations, replacing anticommunism, free trade or democratic self-determination as the current, front-line goal of human societies.[21] The enthusiasm and commitment generated by the Earth Summit, therefore, is obviously a big plus.

Author David Hunt, on the other hand, while he expects peace and ecology to walk hand-in-hand and to unite the world for common survival, warns against those forces which could prepare the way for a single world government under the biblically predicted "Antichrist" of the "last times."[22]

From a more immediate perspective, however, the UN development officers present at Brazil were particularly pleased and impressed by four areas of general agreement among the delegates, linking poverty and environmental issues and showing that preserving the environment is not necessarily an added cost but an investment in the future. Most governments are moving with determination to conserve resources and to cooperate in environmental protection.

"There is greater understanding of the issues and greater recognition that environment and development are two sides of the same sustainable coin. UNCED (United Nations Conference on Environment and Development)," their report boldly states, "is the beginning of a new era in which environment and development are brought together."[23]

If this optimistic assessment of the Earth Summit proves accurate, it is due in part to the careful preparation given to the conference by the UNEP staff in Nairobi. UNEP produced an overview of the state of the global environment that was superbly organized and provides the most concise and authoritative summary available. It is called *Saving our Planet: Challenges and Hopes*, and was published in Nairobi, Kenya, in 1992.[24] Although I have used other sources, many of my observations about the status of Planet Earth come from it.

The alarming surge in global population growth

No current ecological problem is more alarming than the surge of global population growth. The 1990s will witness the largest average annual increases to world population in history. The quickening pace of this frenzied, exponential growth reminds us of the mesmerizing, musical buildup of Ravel's "Bolero."

Loren Wilkinson points out that if the human population

had increased at its current rate from the beginning, God would have had to create Adam and Eve in A.D. 772![25]

Gore puts it in equally dramatic terms. "In the course of one human lifetime—mine—the world population will increase from two to more than nine billion, and it is already more than halfway there."[26]

Experts generally expect that by the year 2010 there will be approximately 7 billion people on the earth. After that, the optimists among demographers expect growth to slow until the world population reaches a stable level of 10.5 billion one hundred years later (2110).[27]

Population growth has already stabilized in the developed countries and in some of those still in the process of development. But in Africa, it continues to hold at close to three percent per year—far too high for comfort.

"The industrialized world," states the UNEP document, "has found that development is the best means of population control. In fact, population growth, development and a productive environment form the three points of a triangle. Progress cannot be made in any one area unless progress is made in the other two."[28]

This may be an oversimplification of the problem. Despite all the development efforts—official and non-governmental—of the past generation, the population growth rate continues to be frightening. We still have so much to learn about development—about what works and what does not work—that we cannot yet afford any complacency.

In fact, the current Somalia famine is highlighting for us the inadequacy of our development programs to date. In my opinion, this is because true development is holistic and is the handmaiden of evangelism.

Development without Christ and his saving and changing power cannot predictably turn people and societies around to make them frugal, unselfish and prosperous. We need to keep our priorities in order. Jesus said, ". . . seek first [God's] kingdom and his righteousness, and all these things will be given to you as well" (Matt.6:33, NIV).

Women a key factor in slowing population growth

The other key social factor to slowing population growth is the provision of adequate health, freedom and education for women. "Without radical improvements in the status of women," the UNEP report goes on to say, "family planning cannot succeed. And this [improvement] cannot be achieved without development."[28]

According to the UNEP report, the most telling and tragic indicator of poverty is the high infant mortality rates. There are still 34 developing countries in which more than one in ten children dies before he or she reaches the age of five. This creates an economic and emotional "demand" for more children. Parents will desire smaller families only when they believe more of their children will survive.[28]

The oppression of women does not affect women alone. In many Third World countries the women are not only the wives and mothers, but also the gardeners and providers of the household. Their low productivity is an important factor in individual and national poverty.

The impact of women on child-rearing is obvious. Women's knowledge about nutrition, health, disease and parenting intimately affects their children's development. Ignorance about breast-feeding, for example, weaning foods or treatment of diarrhea contributes directly to malnutrition and infant mortality. As long as infant mortality is excessive, parents feel the need for more children in the home.

And so—paradoxically—efforts to keep children alive and healthy constitute one of the best keys, in the long run, to reducing population growth rates.

Air pollution in its many forms

When a baby is born and emerges from its mother's womb, the first demand of its little body is for air. Next to life itself, no resource is so important to us as the air we breathe. If we are deprived of air, or if it is replaced by smoke, gas or noxious fumes—we die!

Air pollution comes in many forms, but four pollutants are particularly important: sulfur oxides, emitted mainly by power stations and industry; nitrogen oxides, emitted by power stations, industry and vehicles; hydrocarbons and carbon monoxide, emitted mainly by vehicles; and soot and dust, known technically as suspended particulate matter (SPM), found everywhere where fuels are burned or winds blow.[29]

According to GEMS (Global Environmental Monitoring System), nearly 900 million urban residents are exposed to unhealthy levels of sulfur oxides and more than one billion people are exposed to excessive dust and soot. Air quality is currently "unacceptable" in 16 of the world's largest cities.[30]

Perhaps it is fortunate that petrochemical smog is visible and palpable, so the industrial countries are learning that they must clean up their act. Yet so vast is the atmosphere, and so marvelous in its self-renewing capability, that we pay little or no attention to much of the less apparent global air pollution that is dangerously affecting vegetation and human health.

Air pollution is truly an international problem. Manmade political borders have little impact on the winds and currents of the earth's weather machine. This is a powerful force to unite humankind in a battle against excessive production of carbon dioxide, carbon monoxide, sulfur oxides, nitrogen oxides and suspended particulate matter. Largely spewed out by the industrialized countries, these noxious fumes cause acid rain and adversely affect the elderly, children and those who have respiratory and heart conditions.

In some countries, notably Sweden, the authorities have limed acidified lakes and forest areas to counteract acid rain. Yet the more economical and reasonable approach is to prevent the emission of acid-forming gases at their sources (see chapter 12).

The reduction of the ozone layer

The skies are not just conveyers of the oxygen we breathe. A thin veil of ozone, 25 to 40 kilometers above the earth's surface, protects life below from the portion of the sun's ultraviolet radiation that would otherwise damage many forms of life. Chemicals released on the surface of the earth—notably the chlorofluorocarbons (CFCs) widely used in refrigeration, aerosols and as cleaners in many industries—are damaging this ozone veil.

The first signs of damage to the ozone layer came when scientists discovered a gigantic hole above Antarctica that formed each spring and filled up later in the year. Under pressure from UNEP, the world community began to take steps in 1977 to limit and phase out the production and consumption of CFCs. However, the current level of atmospheric chlorine—which caused the hole—is now two and a half times greater than it was in 1970.[31]

Each one percent reduction in ozone is likely to cause an increase of about two percent in ultraviolet radiation (UV-B). The resulting exposure to UV-B reduces the effectiveness of the body's immune system—increasing disease rates—and produces eye cataracts and skin cancer. UV-B can severely damage plants and aquatic organisms, possibly reducing food production and fish stocks.[32]

As we have seen here, (and will see in chapter 12), we can trace much of the pollution of our air and skies to modern industry. Modern industry produces environmental problems everywhere. It consumes 37 percent of the world's energy and emits 50 percent of the world's carbon dioxide, 90 percent of the world's sulfur oxides and nearly all the toxic chemicals now threatening the ozone layer.[33]

Every year, industry produces 2,100 million tons of solid waste and 338 million tons of hazardous waste.[34] Radioactive waste is expected to stockpile by the year 2000 in the amount of one million cubic meters.[35]

It is true that we are making some progress in the right direction in some of these high-risk areas, but the continuing functionality of the earth's life cycles and ecosystems is far from being assured.

Little drops of water—but too few?

As one of life's most common denominators, water is truly amazing.

To begin with, it is the stuff of which poetry is made. We rhapsodize about babbling brooks, trickling streams, rushing rivers, pounding waves, soaring fountains and thundering waterfalls. For the Christian, water is the symbol of birth (John 3:5), rebirth (Eph. 5:26) and life eternal (Rev. 22:1, 17).

But water is far more practical than it is aesthetic. Among other things, it brings regeneration to arid soils, purging to polluted rivers, moisture to withering vegetation and the sparkle of sustaining life and beauty to almost every part of nature's abundance.

Water, in some form, is virtually ubiquitous. It covers almost three-fourths of the earth's surface and composes more than two-thirds of the corporeal substances we call our bodies.

It is also the elemental ingredient of the earth's vast weather machine and climate control systems. Other components, of course, are not insignificant—the solar energy that powers the process, the thermal currents in the ocean and the jet streams in the sky that distribute the weather around the globe.

But water is the fundamental ingredient and balancing factor. It moderates the heat and tempers the cold, lending stability to the atmosphere. It travels in clouds, precipitates in rain, crystallizes in snow and ice, flows in creeks and rivers, serves patiently in lakes and wetlands.

Water's ubiquity is deceptive

Water seems, indeed, to be everywhere. But this ubiquity is deceptive. Only 6 percent of the earth's water is fresh. Ninety-four percent is in its salty oceans.[36] This 94 percent is not unimportant. On the contrary, it is vital to our well-being. Yet we have assaulted it atrociously by over-fishing, oil spills, damage to coral banks and pollution of coastal waters. But its direct value to us is limited until it becomes a part of the planet's freshwater hydrological cycle.

The existing reserves of fresh water—the 6 percent—would still be much more than we need, except that almost a third of this fresh water is locked into glaciers and polar ice caps, and much of the rest is underground—some of it too far below the surface to exploit.

At any one time, this leaves us with only a tiny portion of the planet's moisture—less than one percent—in the atmosphere, on the earth's surface, or under it that human beings and animals can use as fresh water.

Furthermore, this tiny portion is not evenly distributed. In many places it is already scarce. And an exploding human population, linked to massive agricultural and industrial expansion, makes per capita water reserves a problem of severe urgency.

It is the reduced fresh water reserves—our "hydrological capital"—on which I choose to focus here. Before this decade ends, the shortages may cause wars in the Middle East, more famine in the sub-Sahara and economic pain in the southwestern U.S.—to name only a few of the many areas of stress. It is urgent that we address the planet's water problems, for our survival and well-being depend on our solving them.

From our human perspective, the most important water in the world is the approximately 500,000 cubic kilometers that is sucked up every year into the atmosphere by natural evaporation and transpiration—86 percent of it from the oceans and 14 percent from forests, vegetation and land areas.[37] While it is being carried as clouds, this water is purified and precipitated again upon the earth—both land and sea—in the form of rain, sleet or snow.

In this process, the planet's land masses give up approximately 70,000 cubic kilometers of moisture for "recycling," but gain

110,000 through precipitation. This is what sustains all natural life on earth, including that of the human race.[38] It is the hydrological capital that we must be careful not to overspend, lest we develop an irreversible deficit.

Much of the planet's annual rainfall that falls on land surfaces runs off again into the sea. But there is still more than enough water retained in the soil, in trees, in aquifers, lakes and river systems to sustain human life comfortably—that is, there would be if it were not for the wanton waste and destructive practices of humankind, our careless pollution of rivers, lakes and aquifers and our annihilation of rain forests.

All around the world, fresh water is suffering such enormous loss in both quantity and quality that one leading ecologist predicts a global water crisis before the twenty-first century has even begun.

In a recent book entitled *Last Oasis: Facing Water Scarcity*, Sandra Postel, vice president of Worldwatch Institute, compares the pending water crisis to the oil crunch of the 1970s. Twenty-six countries, she says, already have more people than their water supplies can adequately support.

Where does all the water go?

Why is this? Where does all the water go?

Generally, we can say that 69 percent of it is used for farming, 23 percent for industry and 8 percent for domestic purposes.[39] The problem is that the combined use of water worldwide in 1990 was more than double that of 1950. By the year 2000 water usage is expected to have almost quadrupled over the last half of the century.

Obviously, we have a supply-side problem. The traditional solution has been to call out the engineers to dig canals, to lay pipelines, to construct dams and reservoirs. The Romans built their aqueducts, the Incas designed their mountainside conduits, modern science favors massive dams—TVA, Boulder, Aswan. These dams store water while providing a measure of flood control and generating electricity as well.

But the price has been high in condemned farmland, eroded watersheds and depletion of species. We are still losing the water consumption race. Water tables continue to drop. Aquifers continue to be depleted. Our hydrological resources continue to diminish.

The solution to our problem is not to increase the supply. This is not usually cost-effective. Rather, it is to practice conservation—to use wisely the abundant resources available to us, to avoid waste and contamination. We need to move from the individualistic, frontier mentality of selfish abundance to the neighborly mentality of stewardship and sharing.

The "frontier mentality" of selfish abundance

Much of the world today—and especially the U.S. and other countries of the Americas—is trapped in what we can call a "frontier mentality." Only a few generations ago, when our great-grandparents forged their trail westward across America, they encountered a nature that was bounteous and prolific. The forests were endless, the buffalo herds were too large to count, the lakes and rivers were pristine and overflowing.

If our ancestors needed meat they shot it. If they needed fur they trapped it. If they needed wood they chopped it. Land was theirs for the taking. Water was theirs for the drawing. Trout and bass were theirs for the fishing. Gold and silver were theirs for the mining. Their cattle grazed on public lands.

Everything was free and abundant. There were no limits or restrictions. They could hunt, trap and farm without bothering anyone or being bothered by anyone else.

Theirs was the frontier mentality, and we have inherited most of it. Only since the beginning of this century have governments imposed hunting and fishing licenses and limits, with public parks and preserves established. Even today, the price of lumber is fixed mostly by the cost of logging, the price of water mostly by the cost of piping it.

We still think that natural resources are free. We have not adjusted our mental parameters to the concept of stewardship or to the ethics of sharing.

Translated into hydrological terms, this means that we are still alarmingly careless about how we use water. We let the sprinklers run, leave the faucets open, waterlog the soil and water-cool our machinery as if the water we use is an inexhaustibly abundant resource.

The fact is, there is just not enough of it anymore. If that seems difficult to believe, just ask the residents of Phoenix and Tucson in Arizona, the farmers of California's San Joaquin Valley, the people of Saudi Arabia, of Egypt, of Sudan.

The shortage, however, is due not simply to the inadequacy of supply. Pollution has increased even faster than consumption, aggravating this shortage. To understand our problem of water quantity and quality, we need to look at water in agriculture, in industry and in the domestic context.

While only 16 percent of the world's cropland is irrigated—rainfall waters the remaining 84 percent—the irrigated portion produces 36 percent of the world's food. Many countries rely on such sources for more than half their food supply.[40]

This becomes important when you realize that during most of the earth's modern history, its irrigated areas have grown faster than the population. The result has been more and better food. But that trend is now reversing.

In 1978, according to Sandra Postel, the amount of irrigated land per capita peaked at 48 hectares for every thousand people and has fallen nearly six percent since that time.[41] No doubt this is due to mushrooming population growth and we already feel it in food shortages and famines. It may also be because anywhere from 50-75 percent of the water used in irrigation does not reach the target for which it is diverted.

Recovering some of the water deficit

In time, we could well recover some of the resulting water deficit by traditional, large-scale dams and irrigation projects with a high per-hectare cost. But the greatest need exists in areas like sub-Saharan Africa, which do not offer cost-effective potential for such projects and where the farmers are among the poorest in the world.

65

For them, low cost and low-tech development of water sources and irrigation techniques is probably the best solution. Shallow wells, economical pumps, drip irrigation, strips of plastic between rows to conserve moisture in the soil, traditional terracing, retaining walls and other procedures can offer hope.

Recycling waste water is another important option for more populous areas. Better matching of water quality to different uses can make each gallon more valuable.

"By far the greatest gains lie in redirecting water used in cities and towns for a second use on farms," declares ecologist Postel.[42] Most waste water contains nutrients that belong on the land.

"By using municipal water supplies twice—once for domestic use and again for irrigation—would-be pollutants become valuable fertilizers," Postel explains, "rivers and lakes are protected from contamination, the irrigated land boosts crop production, and the reclaimed water becomes a reliable, local supply."

Israel is the country that leads the world in reuse of waste water. About 70 percent of the nation's sewage is reprocessed to irrigate 19,000 hectares of farmland and considerable further expansion is on the books. [43]

But water-short areas everywhere are working on solutions. Los Angeles plans to reuse 40 percent of its municipal waste water within 20 years. Tucson and Phoenix are also experimenting with recycling and water swapping agreements.

The City Council of Pasadena, California, took only four minutes recently to approve a contract with the neighboring cities of Glendale and Los Angeles for the purchase of recycled sewage water at $25 per acre-foot and piping it 20 miles to irrigate its parks and golf courses. (An acre-foot is roughly the amount of water needed to fill the Pasadena Rose Bowl one foot deep.)

The Metropolitan Water District charges Pasadena $385 per acre-foot for "new" water, so the City Council didn't have to spend time in debate. It signed up fast. By the end of the decade, it is estimated that reclaimed sewage will replace 15 percent of the city's total water usage.[44]

St. Petersburg, Florida, is unique among U.S. cities and sets a bench mark for the rest of the nation. It has two water distribution systems—one for drinking and most household uses, and another with treated waste water for irrigating lawns, parks, roadsides and for other functions that do not require potable quality. The recycled water costs about a third as much as the potable water and cuts down on lawn fertilizer costs as well because of the nutrients it contains. The city reuses all its waste water and discharges none into lakes and streams.

Water contamination is a major concern of the UN and its agencies. Several of them (UNEP, WHO, WMO and UNESCO) are linked in a project called GEMS/WATER. GEMS (Global Environmental Monitoring Service) consists of 344 stations in 59 countries. Of these, 240 monitor rivers, 43 monitor lakes and 61 are ground-water stations. They collect data on about 50 different parameters of water quality, including all kinds of contaminants.[45]

GEMS reports show that we can describe 10 percent of the earth's rivers as polluted. Run-off of fertilizers and pesticides from agricultural lands, industrial waste and untreated sewage are the principal culprits, in that order. Nitrates from fertilizers and feedlot waste have caused the contamination of ground water in many countries and have brought it close to the danger level.

Industry is responsible for heavy metal contaminants and for hazardous waste. These ultimately find their way up the food chain to accumulate harmfully in human bodies. Industry is also very wasteful of water, which it requires in large quantities. We can generally say that industry possesses a "frontier mentality."

The application of drip irrigation methods

Driving into the city from the Larnaka airport on the island of Cyprus one evening, I was impressed by the large stands of saplings and young trees lining the highway. I asked my host about them.

"They are a part of Cyprus's reforestation program," he told me proudly.

"And why do they look so healthy in the heat of the summer?" I asked.

"They are all watered by drip irrigation," he replied. "We've been borrowing from the technologies developed in Israel. And it's working marvelously."

We can most simply describe drip irrigation as a plastic hose running through an orchard or garden with a small hole or holes placed at the base of each tree or plant. This provides a slow and constant delivery of water only where it is needed. Because trees are usually planted several meters apart, the watering is very precise and economical.

Cyprus now leads the world in the application of drip irrigation techniques. Seventy-one percent of its irrigated farmland used "micro-irrigation" in 1991, according to information cited by Sandra Postel. Israel is next, with 48.7 percent.[46]

"Micro-irrigation includes primarily drip (surface and subsurface) methods and micro sprinklers," Postel explains. Israel's irrigated lands have been cut back heavily since 1986 due to drought. Except for Jordan (21.1 percent), no other countries have ventured heavily into the use of this technology, and worldwide employment of micro-irrigation represents only 0.7 percent of all cultivated lands.[47] There is certainly room for massive expansion here.

The worldwide water crisis is a very present reality, and one that we must address on many fronts. Perhaps most urgent, however, is the need to mature and move up the ladder from a frontier mentality to that of good stewards and friendly neighbors.

9

Tracking our vanishing species

"Look! Over there!" Carlos said excitedly. "Do you see that black shadow at the edge of the water?"

We were a full twenty-five yards away, and the pale moonlight on the white beach was not enough for us to distinguish any details. But the big black splotch was unmistakable.

"She's a big baby," Carlos added, his voice now more conspiratorial, "but don't move any closer. Her hormones are pumping like mad right now and if she spots us and gets scared, she could easily turn right around and head back into the ocean."

Tracking the leatherback turtle

It was 10:00 p.m. on a February night at Playa Grande, Costa Rica, a broad tidal beach of hard-packed sand. About four kilometers of this beach is reserved for the nesting habits of the "baula," or leatherback, turtles—the largest turtle species in the world.

We were there as the pampered guests of Tikal Tours of Costa Rica, a pioneer in what is becoming known as "ecotourism." Carlos was our well-informed guide.

He pointed again to the black shadow. "This one looks as though her 'shell'—or her leather back—might be just a bit over a meter long," he told us. "That's a good size, although the largest measured turtle on record is 2.3 meters, and some have claimed to see them even bigger. Of course, the biggest ones are the males," he added, "and they never come back to shore from the time of their birth, so we can't measure them or tag them."

The slowly moving shadow began to take form for us in the pale moonlight. It was as big as a small refrigerator. Our guide had warned us not to get in front of the turtle. Flashlights were prohibited unless they had infrared filters, and flash photos strictly forbidden.

It was still possible, however, to see some movement. The laboring leatherback was literally "swimming" with her flippers on the hard sand—something like crawling on your elbows—and leaving a double trail, etched deep, like that of a tractor. Slowly, and breathing hard, she dragged herself across the beach and up into the low dunes of soft sand where she would bury her eggs.

In a hushed voice, while we sat on the sand and watched the turtle's painstaking progress, Carlos filled us in on the relatively scant information available about this species of turtle.

It is not a tortoise—it has no hands and legs like a land turtle. This one probably weighed about 700 pounds. She resembled a huge, semi-inflated American football, with seven characteristic "seams" stretching the oval length of her back.

"There is a population of perhaps one thousand female turtles that use this beach to lay their eggs—from 50 to 100 at a time—perhaps four or five times each year, during the season that runs from October to March," he said. "Many have been tagged, and have been spotted all over the ocean, as far north as Vancouver."

"What do they feed on?" I asked him.

"Mostly deep-sea jellyfish," was his reply. "They are very strong and graceful swimmers, and have been known to dive as deep as two miles. They can protect themselves from the 'bends' by drawing their blood into the center of their bodies, and they are capable of generating their own body heat—one of the few species of reptile able to do that." It was obvious that our guide held the leatherbacks in great respect and affection.

This one had now reached the dry sand of the dunes and was rocking and flipping herself to form a bowl-like indentation in the sand.

"Come on, carefully," Carlos told us. "Follow me quietly to the back of the turtle, away from her head. Her hormones are now focused on nesting and laying, and our proximity won't bother her," he explained.

The female leatherback lays her eggs

The turtle now lay anchored on a ridge of sand under her head and upper body, spreading her front flippers to achieve maximum stability. While Carlos illuminated the scene from behind with his tiny red flashlight, and we hunched silently around him, the leatherback began her slow ballet.

Shifting her weight to one of her rear flippers, with the other one she scooped out a small fistful of sand. Then she shifted to the other rear flipper, and repeated the movement with her first one. Slowly, carefully, with accuracy and symmetry, she swayed back and forth from one flipper to the other—all 700 pounds of her—until she had scooped out a bucket-sized nest about 20 inches below the surface of the sand.

Then she began dropping her eggs—round, big, sometimes one, sometimes two at a time, with a few much smaller ones to provide packing and protection for the big ones. Carlos sprawled facedown behind her and held one flipper aside so that we could see the eggs plop out—an average of 80 to a nest, I am told.

It was an awe-inspiring sight—almost a religious experience—to watch this massive mother carefully and tenderly lay her eggs, then ease the moist sand back on top of them, a scant fistful at a time, in a continuing ballet of her two rear flippers.

She smoothed, tamped and pressed each stroke with precisely the right effort to ensure the safety of the eggs from predators and the capability of her tiny offspring to hatch and surface when they had completed the sixty days of their incubation. Then she scattered sand, bearing her body scent, over the whole area as she refilled the bowl, camouflaged the site and pushed her way out and back to the ocean—now much farther away with the ebbing tide.

The turtle's breathing was labored and there seemed to be tears in her eyes from the extraordinary exertion that this whole process required of her. There were tears in our eyes, too, as we thought about how God had created and taught this leviathan of the sea to nurture her young with such tenderness and power to ensure the continuation of the species.

When they are hatched, the baby turtles are almost certainly doomed to die young. As their tiny heads break the surface after two months underground—as we watched them do in several spots that night—they often become disoriented and don't arrive at the ocean. In fact, no one knows quite how they do target the ocean. But light, sound—almost anything—can distract them from their course.

The newborn turtles are a gourmet diet for birds, animals, sharks and other fish. There is no assurance of their survival even after they reach the water. It is estimated that their chances of arriving at adulthood are only about one in a thousand, making every egg, and every surviving turtle, precious.

Worldwide, the leatherback leads an endangered existence. Playa Grande is one of the three largest nesting grounds for the baula species. Some ecological balance is being achieved there. But other places are less protected, and only great care and concern by governments and peoples can keep these areas safe not only from natural predators, but from the vicious, the vandals and the merely curious humans who interfere with the turtles' ecosystems.

The diversity of species on our planet

Why so much concern for only one out of many species on earth today, you may ask? Aren't there some 30 million species of life on the planet? What makes the leatherback so important?

No one knows for sure, of course, how many species really do exist. Thirty million may be a good guess. However, scientists have described only 1.4 million, and of these, more than half are insects and 250,000 are plants. Only 41,000 are vertebrates.[48]

While this seems like a lot, we need to balance it against the alarming fact that according to the UNEP, "over 99 percent of the species that have ever existed are now extinct . . . In recent history, humans have had an increasing impact on species extinctions."[49]

As Al Gore points out, ". . . living species of animals and plants are now vanishing around the world one thousand times faster than at any time in the past 65 million years."[50] This is because of the immensely increased human impact on the environment in the last century. We are now losing species at the rate of almost 100,000 each year, half of them from tropical deforestation.[51]

There are a number of valid reasons for focusing—at least for illustrative purposes—on the leatherback as typical of our many endangered species.

To begin with, Playa Grande is in tropical Costa Rica. This is important because any discussion of species must recognize that the distribution is not uniform and that species richness increases from the poles to the equator.

"In one area of about 15 hectares of rain forest in Borneo," states the UNEP report, "about 700 species of trees were identified, as many as in all of North America."[52] We could say the same of Brazil, Guatemala or Madagascar, and many others.

Patterns of land and marine diversity of species increase in the tropics and reach their peak in the tropical forests and coral reefs. Tropical forests cover only 7 percent of the earth's land surface, but contain more than half the species in the entire world. Today 3,956 species are endangered, 3,647 are vulnerable, and 7,240 are considered rare.[53]

We can easily identify four major causes of the loss of species:[54]

1. Habitat loss or modification, such as the reduction of forest areas;

2. Over-exploitation, such as "strip-mining" the oceans with thirty-five-mile-long, fine-mesh drift-nets, or massacring elephants for ivory;

3. Pollution of air and water that the species need for survival; and

4. The impact of introduced exotic species that become predators, competitors or alterers of the natural habitat.

Biodiversity an essential element for healthy survival

Biodiversity appears to be an essential element for the healthy survival of the natural world. Its loss ultimately affects all of us, most specifically and immediately because it reduces the genes available for the continued improvement and maintenance of currently utilized species—such as the more abundant rice of the "green revolution" or disease-resistant fruits and poultry. When we compute the production of grains in financial terms, the introduction of genes from wild plants saves literally billions of dollars per year—and a proportionate number of lives. Worldwide, medicines from wild products are worth some $40 billion per year.[55]

One of the principal responses to the current reduction of species is the establishment of protected areas, like the one at Playa Grande in Costa Rica. By setting aside 500 hectares of its beach and estuaries and 22,000 hectares of adjoining ocean area, Costa Rica has protected the future of the baula turtle and many other botanical and zoological species. The nation has limited the access of intruders to the nesting and mangrove areas. It has given employment as salaried guards and guides to dozens of local former egg-poachers. It has encouraged extensive research and scientific investigation. And it has nurtured a "boomlet" of tourist industry, attracting visitors and their "ecotourist" dollars from all over the world.

An increased awareness of the delicacy of our natural ecosystems and the support and care that they need and deserve is another more important long-term response by the Costa Rican people. All schools provide Costa Rican children with some knowledge of ecology. One of the principal television stations calls itself the "The Ecological Channel." The national park and preserves program leads the world when measured by population percentages.

Costa Rica still has a long way to go, but it is pointing the way to a positive kind of awareness that can find places—like the nesting grounds of the baula turtle—to patch God's garment and help defer the destruction of our earth.

10
Looking forward from Brazil

Despite some political foot-dragging by the U.S. government, the environmentalist-delegates present in Brazil at the Earth Summit of 1992 returned to their 170 home countries in a state of near-euphoria.

The accomplishments, as reported by UN development officers, were indeed numerous and significant.[56]

What did the Earth Summit achieve?

1. The first major achievement was the adoption of the **Río Declaration on Environment and Development**. This was a set of 27 non-binding principles that emphasize the link between environment and development, adopted by consensus.

2. **Agenda 21**. For the first time in the history of the UN the delegates adopted a document of over 800 pages of text by consensus. Agenda 21 will serve as a guide for future action to governments and non-government agencies alike through the next century.

While it is a "universal" document that governments must now adapt to fit each country's needs, Agenda 21 covers development problems, ecological concerns and means for strengthening the role of major groups such as women, youth, indigenous peoples and local authorities.

Just to review the document's content is to sense an encouraging indicator of the increase in public awareness and training in environmental issues over the twenty-year span of UNEP's (United Nations Environmental Programme) lifetime.

Its coverage includes: eradication of poverty, consumption patterns, freshwater resources, solid waste management, urban pollution, land resources, energy, sustainable agriculture and rural development, forests, management of fragile ecosystems, biological diversity, biotechnology, atmosphere, oceans and seas, toxic chemicals, hazardous and radioactive wastes.

3. **Global warming convention**. When this is ratified by the signatory governments, it will be a legally binding treaty aimed at lowering emissions of carbon dioxide, methane and other greenhouse gases into the atmosphere. A built-in review process will allow for early revisions.

4. **Biodiversity convention**. This also is a legally binding treaty aimed at halting the destruction of biological diversity and at introducing standards of conduct in the sharing of research, information, profits and technology in genetic resources.

The U.S. did not sign this convention because of reservations about clauses dealing with the protection of intellectual property and the sharing of profits related to biotechnology development. Many nations considered this position as a major *faux pas* by the U.S., exhibiting political subservience to big business pressures.

That the U.S. did not sign in Río was perceived by some as weakening the impact of the convention. That most other major powers did sign, however, gives the convention great stature, and U.S. endorsement was later forthcoming from the Clinton administration. Under the convention—still to be ratified by each signatory nation—each nation must keep inventories and design plans to protect endangered species as well as to protect areas important for biodiversity.

5. **Forestry principles**: "This was the surprise of the Earth Summit," according to the report of the UN development officers. Unexpected by many, last-minute political dynamics at the conference made the statement on forestry principles possible.

Although this is a non-binding document, it is nonetheless important because it recognizes that forests are essential for economic development as well as for carbon dioxide sequestration, the preservation of species and the maintenance of equilibrium in the global climate.

6. **Desertification and drought**. The conference also finalized a declaration on *Managing Fragile Ecosystems: Combating Desertification and Drought*. This consists of six program areas aimed at reducing the impact of the problems of desertification and drought in arid, semi-arid and dry sub-humid areas.

The delegates also decided to establish an Intergovernmental Negotiating Committee to elaborate an international convention before June 1994, with Africa especially in mind.

7. **Institutional arrangements**. The most important outcome was the agreement to create a high-level Commission on Sustainable Development. This commission will report to the General Assembly and has the important task of monitoring the progress of the implementation of Agenda 21 and its financial provisions. A secretariat supports this commission, and the secretary-general will decide the locations and composition of the secretariat.

The delegates also formed an "Earth Council" to implement, support and affirm the Sustainable Development Commission. Chaired by renowned ecologist Maurice Strong, the coordinator of the Brazil Summit and founding director of UNEP, the Earth Council consists of 21 environmentalists representing different states selected by geographical distribution.

Funded not by the UN, but by private foundations, the Earth Council is a "people's network" to serve as a catalyst to coordinate and encourage NGOs, industry, business and scientific communities. It will also provide for the active involvement of organs, programs and organizations of the UN system, international financial institutions and other relevant intergovernmental organizations. The Earth Council's headquarters are in Costa Rica.

Financial commitments for environmental assistance

8. **Financial resources and mechanisms**. Many went away from Río disappointed because of what they considered a lack of resource commitments by donors. Consequently, they hardly noticed those delegations that made indicative pledges.

For example, Japan promised to increase its environmentally-related development assistance up to a five-year total of $7.5 billion. The European Economic Community (EEC) announced that it would jointly commit $4 billion to help in the implementation of Agenda 21. The EEC gave no schedule for disbursement, however, nor was there any indication of where the money would come from.

France promised to double its funding level for the GEF (Global Environment Facility). Germany called for a tripling of the GEF funding (from its current $1.3 billion to approximately $4 billion over a period of three years), and promised to maintain its share of that sum. The United Kingdom supported the doubling of the GEF to $2-$3 billion a year.

Canada announced that it would spend more on sustainable development in the next five years than the $1.3 billion it had spent in the last five. Canada also promised that through its International Development Agency (CIDA), it would eliminate $145 million of debt in Latin America in exchange for sustainable development projects.

The U.S. promised to increase its international environment aid about 66 percent over 1990 levels. The U.S. also spoke of $250 million to aid the world's forests. There were other commitments as well.

The development officers' report points out that "the financial resources and mechanisms chapter 33, widely considered the most important chapter of Agenda 21, sets the framework for the financing of Agenda 21 and other related agreements of UNCED (the Earth Summit) . . . and calls on donor countries to reach the accepted target of 0.7 percent of GNP for ODA and calls on the Sustainable Development Commission to monitor the progress towards this target.

"UNDP (United Nations Development Programme) will take a leading role," the report concluded, "in helping developing countries convert these into real sustainable development plans suitable for the implementation of Agenda 21."

Since the current "awareness window" (1960 to 1992) opened, never has the world's environmental crisis received wider and more careful attention than at the Río de Janeiro summit. At the top level of ecological concern, at least, action to reestablish environmental balance is at its most hopeful peak.

It should be apparent by now that we must address many environmental problems at the international level. Pollution, weather, oceans and even rivers do not respect ethno-political boundaries. But that the solution to many ecological problems must depend to some degree on government actions does not mean that as citizens and individuals we can wash our hands of any responsibility.

Governments—at least in democratic nations—will move only under pressure from the voting populace. Environmental awareness across this nation—across any nation—is essential, therefore, if we are to expect official response to the current crisis.

It should be equally apparent, however, that we must also address the problems at every level—international, national, state, county, city, community, church, school, business and home. Only a total effort to protect the environment can make a significant difference.

Personal action can make a difference

Journalism student Diane Tegarden recently wrote an article for my local newspaper. It illustrates the dimensions of capability that each one of us possesses to relieve the pressure on the earth's ecosystems. Each of us in California, she states, "creates approximately 1,259 pounds of waste per year—over one half ton of trash. This can be reduced by 30 percent by following a plan of recycling containers, choosing products that use less packaging and reusing the containers of the products that we buy."[57]

The article goes on to detail how and where we can recycle different items: glass, paper, aluminum, steel, and plastics; giving addresses and detailed instructions related to car batteries, auto freon gas, and yard trimmings; and explaining how to avoid toxic and non-biodegradable household laundry and cleaning products.

"We can make a difference," Tegarden concludes, "but we have to make an effort. Remember, before consumers started boycotting tuna, there was no such thing as 'dolphin-safe tuna.' No matter how small your contribution to the solution of the problem is, it will matter . . . You can make crucial decisions that will help change the world or help bury it."

Articles like this one should appear regularly in every local newspaper to help universalize the movement to protect our ailing environment.

Not only will personal action—and collective effort at the church-school-community level—make a perceptible difference. It is a significant part of the worldwide process of creating awareness. Each local and personal action—every sound ecological decision—serves as a reminder that our environment is in crisis and that God's garment is wearing thin. Only such an awareness can give us the perspective of wise stewardship and obedience that God expects of us today.

11
Action plans and audits

"A Global Marshall Plan" is what Vice President Gore has called his proposal for rescuing the environment from disaster. "If we cannot embrace the preservation of the earth as our new organizing principle," he says, "the very survival of our civilization will be in doubt."[58]

Written before the Earth Summit in Brazil, actions taken by the UN at the UNCED in 1992 have already incorporated or superseded some of Gore's suggestions. For example, the establishment of the high-level Commission on Sustainable Development, as well as the creation of the Earth Council, fulfilled his proposal for a "Stewardship Council" to monitor global environmental agreements. Generally, the UN appears to have risen above expectations and has shown that much of the world is more than ready to listen to proposals of the "Marshall Plan" type.

Admittedly, the difficulties of involving the wealthy nations of the world in support of such a plan are enormous. The U.S. is dragging its feet, Japan is insensibly reluctant, and Europe has its hands full with its own integration. But doing nothing can turn out to be far more costly than making immediate sacrifices.

Gore's five strategic goals for rescuing the environment

Gore puts forward five strategic goals which are worth quoting directly from his book:[59]

1. The first strategic goal should be the stabilizing of world population, with policies designed to create in every nation of the world the conditions necessary for the so-called demographic transition—the historic and well-documented change from a dynamic equilibrium of high birth rates and death rates to a stable equilibrium of low birth rates and death rates.

   This change has taken place in most of the industrial nations (which have low rates of infant mortality and high rates of literacy and education) and in virtually none of the developing nations (where the reverse is true).

2. The second strategic goal should be the rapid creation and development of environmentally appropriate technologies—especially in the fields of energy, transportation, agriculture, building construction, and manufacturing—capable of accommodating sustainable economic progress without the concurrent degradation of the environment. These new technologies must then be quickly transferred to all nations—especially those in the Third World, which should be allowed to pay for them by discharging the various obligations they incur as participants in the Global Marshall Plan.

3. The third strategic coal should be a comprehensive and ubiquitous change in the economic 'rules of the road' by which we measure the impact of our decisions on the environment. We must establish—by global agreement—a system of economic accounting that assigns appropriate values to the ecological consequences of both routine choices in the marketplace by individuals and companies and larger, macroeconomic choices by nations.

4. The fourth strategic goal should be the negotiation and approval of a new generation of international agreements which will embody the regulatory frameworks, specific prohibitions, enforcement mechanisms, cooperative planning, sharing arrangements, incentives, penalties, and mutual obligations necessary to make the overall plan a success. These agreements must be especially sensitive to

the vast differences of capability and need between developed and undeveloped nations.

5. The fifth strategic goal should be the establishment of a cooperative plan for educating the world's citizens about our global environment—first by the establishment of a comprehensive program for researching and monitoring the changes now under way in the environment in a manner that involves the people of all nations, especially students; and second, through a massive effort to disseminate information about local, regional and strategic threats to the environment. The ultimate goal of this effort would be to foster new patterns of thinking about the relationship of civilization to the global environment.

   Each of these goals is closely related to all of the others, and all should be pursued simultaneously within the larger framework of the Global Marshall Plan.

   Finally, the plan should have as its more general, integrating goal the establishment, especially in the developing world, of the social and political conditions most conducive to the emergence of sustainable societies—such as social justice (including equitable patterns of land ownership); a commitment to human rights; adequate nutrition, health care and shelter; high literacy rates; and greater political freedom, participation and accountability. Of course, all specific policies should be chosen as part of serving the central organizing principle of saving the global environment.

With the proposal of each of these goals for rescuing the environment, Gore suggests a series of tactical actions for implementation—some for application in the U.S. and others for global adoption. The more they are studied, the more feasible they seem to become.

At first perusal, because they often run counter to entrenched practices and vested interests, Gore's proposals seem unattainably idealistic. But even if they fail, any attempt to implement them should increase global awareness of the environmental crisis—which is positive. As it becomes more obvious that humanity's survival depends on some such intelligent cooperation—which happened in the banning of nuclear weapons, for example—the world powers may yet decide to live together rather than to die separately.

Gore's third strategy—to undertake a "comprehensive and ubiquitous change in the economic 'rules of the road,' by which we measure the impact of our decisions on the environment"—holds special appeal at this time.

"The hard truth," as he points out, "is that our economic system is partially blind."[60] It fails to see and measure the waste we produce. It ignores the depreciation and increasing scarcity of raw materials. And it totally overlooks its own trail of pollution and negative impact.

Auditing organizations for their natural and human resources

For many years it has been my conviction that every industry, governmental agency, public institution and private business should be required to undergo a regular audit—not only of its operational profit and loss and its capital assets, but of its natural and human resources as well.

The basic building blocks of the U.S. economy are (1) people, or producers, (2) material resources, or raw materials and (3) money, or cash and invested capital. We have laws governing the use and exploitation of all three of these factors, but, oddly enough, the general practice is to report annually and receive an audit only on the use of finances. We conveniently overlook the use or exploitation of employees and the utilization or consumption of environmental materials, along with the waste they produce.

Why should we audit a business solely on how it manages its money—but not on how it treats the people who do its work or on how it abuses its natural resources?

For example, an audit of "FACTORY A" can show by its profit and loss statement that it is a profitable operation, and therefore a "good investment." But in reality, it may be forcing its people to work in unhealthy conditions and may be spewing pollution into the local rivers. This does not show up in its audit.

Gore appropriately recommends that we should change the definition of GNP (Gross National Product) to include environmental costs and benefits, and that we should adjust the definition of productivity to reflect calculations of environmental improvement or decline.[61]

The triple audit gives a more complete picture

Maybe that is where it should start. But we should also apply this new perspective on the economy—which is triangulated from the three major perspectives of (1) the environment, (2) the producers, and (3) the investors of capital—to the practice of audits. Otherwise, the spectrum is incomplete and the picture is distorted.

Perhaps one reason why the triple audit has not become a general practice is that each of the perspectives has a different time horizon. Financial audits have usually been annual—although in some cases the 12-month fiscal year is inconveniently short, and a 24-month "year" might be more economical and appropriate.

We can probably measure environmental factors with more accuracy (and a more correct dollar value) in a period of 36 to 60 months (three to five years). Human or employee factors may need even more time to measure improvement or decline in physical and mental health and productivity. But we must build the provision for such periodical audits into the system.

It is true that the government requires an "environmental impact" study of new projects, especially construction projects. But this is simply a good guess about the future. Once the original project has been studied and approved, there is no built-in provision for a periodic review of its ecological impact.

In the long run, capital, or economic resources, are no more essential to business and industry than are personnel and environmental resources. This means that an adequate, regular audit should embrace all three factors.

Environmental awareness brings financial rewards

Such a new-perspective review may even prove to be of great benefit to the businesses and institutions that are audited.

Environmentalist Gil Friend, of San Francisco, states that "a growing number of business leaders have recognized that economic health, whether of individual companies or the national economy, isn't in conflict with environmental quality. It thrives on it."[62]

One company (3M) has saved nearly two-thirds of a billion dollars, Friend declares, on its pioneering "pollution prevention" program. Even the American Chemical Society has made the point that environmental improvement programs are paying off financially.

At the national level, claims Friend, "if we simply matched Japan's level of energy efficiency, the United States would spend $230 billion a year on energy instead of the current $450 billion." That savings is equal to a big chunk of our federal deficit.

In another newspaper column, Friend reports on many companies that are beginning to approach the annual audit concept. Dow Chemical Corp., for example, now charges its plant supervisors for waste management costs.[63]

"Without proper allocation," he reports, "a company might mis-allocate resources to activities with high waste-disposal costs. One answer is to make each business activity be responsible in a profit-and-loss way for the waste they generate, so each business unit manager says, 'This is really affecting my bottom line.'"

"When you make sure that everybody realizes the real costs," Stanford economist Jeremy Bulow is quoted as saying, "you're much better off."[64] Equally important is the elimination of hidden subsidies in business accounting practices. The clear definition of these factors is an essential element of any quality control program and crucial also to a frugal and efficient use of resources.

A vice president of Bain & Company, one of the world's largest consulting firms, recently told me that some of their consultants are working on the development of an environmental balance sheet. This would certainly be another valuable step towards filling the void I have mentioned.

We come back, therefore, to the concept of awareness—for investors, for managers, for the populace, and for CEOs. Only when we are aware of the facts will we discard our blinders and alter our accounting to reflect the true values and impact of waste and pollution. Then, and only then, will our children and grand-children be free of the environmental impoverishment we are now passing on to them.

12

The case of the conscientious CEO

W hen gasoline was rationed in Costa Rica during World War II, it frequently became my task to drive the Dodge station wagon to the National Liquor Factory and there fill the tank halfway with pure alcohol. I then took it to the gas station and used our coupons to top off the tank with regular gasoline.

This routine became necessary not because of the local smog problem, but because of the wartime scarcity of gasoline. It was also a foretaste, so to speak, of what may become common practice as the reduction of contaminating fossil fuels in highway vehicles becomes increasingly mandatory.

Toxic emissions and motor vehicles

According to current legislation, two percent of the new cars sold in the U.S. state of California must be completely free of toxic emissions by 1998; that quota must rise to 10 percent by 2003. That means that one out of every ten cars will be electrically powered, since by today's technologies only an electric motor is emission-free. In addition, many companies have already converted buses and car fleets to natural gas, which is much more friendly to the environment than gasoline.

Will today's gasoline-powered automobile become tomorrow's dinosaur—a lost figure of history? Not quite. But the twenty-first century will have to become a century of automotive innovation if the car is to continue to be our favorite mode of transportation.

The problem is complex. There are probably too many vehicles cluttering the roads already. The U.S. boasts almost 400 cars for every 500 people. That is twice as many as Japan, almost four times as many as Europe and ten times as many as the rest of the world. Today's motor vehicle "population" of 500 million is expected to double to one billion early in the next century.[65]

Transport is indeed a greedy consumer of both land and energy. In developed countries the highways have doubled over the past two decades. Transport consumes 30 percent of the world's commercial energy.[66]

Cleaner fuels, fortunately, are gaining acceptance—which gives hope for some atmospheric improvement. For example, one-third of Brazil's cars can run on pure ethanol, and many more on an ethanol-petrol mix, similar to the makeshift World War II practice that I mentioned at the beginning of this chapter. Italy, Argentina, Australia, Indonesia, Japan, New Zealand, Pakistan and Thailand are beginning to use natural gas.

Manufacturers have also made major strides in improving gasoline mileage. The average vehicle in the U.S. now uses half as much fuel as it did 20 years ago. And the elimination of lead from gasoline has been an important step.

However, motor vehicles—or rather, the transport sector—continue to be major polluters of the atmosphere, generating 60 percent of carbon monoxide (CO_1) emissions, 42 percent of nitrogen oxides, 40 percent of hydrocarbons, 13 percent of particulates and 3 percent of sulfur oxides.

Although many automobiles have smog-controlling catalytic converters, they still produce large amounts of carbon dioxide—15 percent of the anthropogenic CO_2 in our atmosphere being attributable to the transport sector. And CO_2 is a key factor in the global warming which threatens our planet.[67]

So do we move totally to electric automobiles?

It's not quite that simple. Because, while electricity is easily controllable and extremely convenient, it is far from cheap, either in dollars or in environmental impact. The vehicle itself, at least in its present semi-experimental model, costs about $100,000 to manufacture. Also, electricity requires large generating facilities, extensive transporting power lines and is difficult to store.[68]

Unfortunately, we cannot satisfy our appetite for electric power by the "clean" sources of water and wind. We must supplement it by fossil-fueled power generating plants—which also disgorge into the skies huge amounts of carbon dioxide—or by nuclear plants that leave hazardous waste.

Will American ingenuity find a way out of this dilemma?

Christian convictions and environmental responsibility

One striking experience has been that of Dennis Bakke, president of the AES Corporation in Arlington, Virginia (U.S.A.). He has discovered a convergence between his Christian convictions and his environmental responsibility.

AES is in the business of developing, owning and operating power stations—electricity generating plants. Somewhere between 55 percent and 80 percent of all the carbon dioxide produced by human activities comes from burning fossil fuels—much of it to produce electric power.[69] When this factor was added to the rapid deforestation of the earth, Bakke and his associates could see that their industry was accelerating—not moderating—the degradation of the atmosphere. And this bothered them deeply.

The problem was not new, of course. They knew that CO_2 was increasing so fast that the charts looked like an elevator shaft—almost vertical. For centuries the amount of carbon dioxide in the atmosphere had vacillated around 200 ppm (parts per million). With the availability of carbon fuels, however, it has increased rapidly and is expected to reach 600 ppm in less than 40 years.[70]

"What does this mean?" Bakke and his colleagues asked themselves. "And what can we do about it?"

Carbon dioxide is a natural part of our ecosphere. All animal life produces it. So do volcanoes. Particularly in their growing stages, trees and plants capture it and convert it by photosynthesis into carbon and oxygen. They store the carbon in wood and fossil, and release the oxygen into the atmosphere for life-sustaining reuse.

Production and recycling are normal processes in the earth's ecosystems. But human impact in recent decades has upset the equilibrium. The large-scale combustion of wood and fossil fuels releases carbon dioxide in greater quantities than before. The industrial revolution (and the generation of electricity) has accelerated output in unprecedented proportions.

Excessive carbon dioxide and the damage it causes

Bakke and company realized that an increased production of CO_2 may be having the effect of trapping solar heat within the earth's ecosystem, not allowing it to reflect normally back into space. This is the still unproven theory of many environmental scientists. They theorize that the planet becomes a greenhouse, with gradually rising temperatures and corresponding changes in climate and living conditions. It conceivably could end up by melting polar ice caps, raising ocean levels and temperatures and causing coastal flooding, along with other less predictable ecological damage.[71]

Under normal conditions, the earth's vast "sinks" compensate for this increase in carbon dioxide, converting it back to carbon and oxygen. The ocean surfaces serve to some degree as sinks, as do the world's forests—especially those in tropical zones where growth is faster. Those in temperate or arctic areas are helpful, but less effective, because the process is most efficient where trees grow quickly. This is why scientists believe that the alarming rate of deforestation in the tropics is rapidly exacerbating the so-called "greenhouse effect," disturbing both ecologists and political leaders alike.

Other scientists scorn the greenhouse effect as melodramatic pop science. They claim that in reality it is probably the cyclic warming of the earth that has led to higher levels of CO_2, rather than the other way around.

Bakke and his associates were not sure about the greenhouse effect, but decided to do something anyway. Like others in their industry, they had already struggled to heal it of some of its contaminating side effects. They were operating three small coal-burning units because coal was a more abundant resource than petroleum. Internal "scrubbers" reduced their toxic output.[72]

Business and industry meet environmental accountability

As they designed their next facility for a spot at Uncasville, on the Thames River in Connecticut (U.S.), they called on all the experience they could muster. A tall chimney—in this case, 386 feet—would move the exhaust away from locally dangerous concentrations.

To keep sulfur dioxide—part of acid rain—out of the emissions, the facility would burn limestone with the coal. A "circulating fluidized bed boiler" in a 110-foot, steel-encased tower, would control the reaction between the coal and limestone to produce a non-toxic fertilizer to be used to reclaim land scarred by strip-mining.

"Profits aren't really the ultimate goal for us. It's being a good neighbor and being a good citizen," said Bakke. "We are simply being good stewards of the resources available to meet the need for electricity in the world." He might have added, "It's also being a good Christian," because this was a prime factor in the evolution of his own principles.

Bakke co-founded AES with Roger Sant, the firm's CEO and chairman. A major advocate for the environment, Sant had been Bakke's boss in the U.S. Federal Energy Administration. They are of one mind about environmental accountability. "We try to weigh our responsibility with trying to deliver a product to our customers which meets their needs," Bakke added. In this case his own Christian principles coincided with the most intelligent ecological procedures.

But the excessive CO_2 continued to be a problem.

"In making electricity," one AES engineer explained, "you've got a process that pollutes. Our objective was to see what we could do to minimize all types of pollution coming from the plant."

The solution AES ultimately proposed was to plant or conserve trees. The trees' filtering processes would compensate for the disgorging of carbon dioxide into the atmosphere during the anticipated life of each generating plant constructed. AES would match the number of trees with the anticipated emission of pollutants—15 million metric tons of carbon in the carbon dioxide emitted over the 40-year operating life of the Thames River plant. This would call for 52 million trees in a tropical climate.

Trees planted anywhere in the planet's tropical belt would serve the same purpose, because the earth's weather machine of sunshine, winds and ocean currents quickly distributes atmospheric components evenly around the globe. So AES focused on a project in Guatemala proposed by CARE, Inc., an international humanitarian agency.

AES and CARE announced this project in 1988. More recently, when a new coal-burning plant at Barbers Point in Oahu, Hawaii (U.S.A.), was on the drawing boards, Bakke and his team came up with a plan to finance the preservation of a semitropical natural forest in Paraguay, South America.

The project in Guatemala called for planting trees as living fence posts, windbreaks, fruit groves, timber forests and other agriculturally oriented purposes. Conservation is the aim of the project in Paraguay, protecting the varieties and species of jungle life still found in one of the few remaining virgin forests of the area.

A still more recent venture is a $3 million proposal to offset the carbon dioxide output of an AES power plant in Shady Point, Oklahoma (U.S.A.). With the help of the World Resources Institute in Washington, AES chose a joint project proposal by Oxfam America for preserving four jungle areas in the Amazon Basin, one located in Ecuador, one in Peru and two in Bolivia—all close to the border with Brazil. Working with the Coordinating Body of Indigenous Peoples' Organizations (COICA), Oxfam's purpose is to help the people of the Amazon preserve and manage more than a million acres of forest.

Financial costs and program objectives

As valuable as the programs may prove, they are not cheap. In Guatemala, AES is putting up $2 million. In a program that will ultimately involve 40,000 farmers and their families, CARE and the Agency for International Development (AID) are each providing $2 million in cash or in-kind financing. The Guatemalan government is committed to contributing $1.2 million. And the services and training of the 35 Peace Corps volunteers who are working on the project are valued at $7.5 million. That brings the total cost to $10.7 million.

The total cost of the Paraguay "Mbaracayu," as it is called, has yet to be determined by an ongoing inventory of the existing forest. But AES's share of up to $2 million, made as a contribution to The Nature Conservancy of Arlington, Virginia (U.S.A.), has facilitated the purchase of a 225 square mile tract of forest by the Moises Bertoni Foundation in Paraguay.

A major objective is to establish Mbaracayu as a managed nature reserve. The Ache, an indigenous tribe of hunters and gatherers, will help to manage the land and retain the right to traditional uses. The several thousand Ache live in villages surrounding the Mbaracayu.

The forest is also home to 19 distinct plant communities, at least 300 bird species, and a wide variety of threatened and endangered species, including jaguars, tapirs, peccaries, giant armadillos, the rare bush dog, king vultures and macaws.

Economic activities encouraged in the buffer zone of the reserve, such as low-impact agriculture, beekeeping and eco-tourism, will also enlarge the economic options of the Ache, a people who have been in contact with the modern world only since 1976. It will also provide a long-term offset for much of the CO_2 that the plant in Barbers Point, Hawaii, will generate.

The threatened greenhouse effect in the world's atmosphere is still a much-debated issue. But the worst course, experts say, would be to do nothing. That is why they are so impressed by AES' projects. To a certain extent these are symbolic, but they are also courageous.

The World Resource Institute's Gus Speth agrees. Deciding to do something about the carbon dioxide problem—before any law requires it—"is one of the most farsighted and socially responsible decisions a private company has ever made," he says.

13
A fraternity of missionary earthkeepers

Deep in the woods of the U.S. state of Michigan, near the little-known town of Mancelona, north of Detroit, a few unpretentious buildings house the Au Sable Institute of Environmental Studies. Very few people have heard of it, but Christian ecologists all over the world have watched it become an important center for reflection, research and exchange of ideas about the human use of creation.

Under the capable direction of Dr. Calvin DeWitt, professor of environmental studies at the University of Wisconsin in Madison (U.S.A.), the Au Sable Institute has provided a summer setting for graduate students preparing their theses, for lectures and seminars on environmental subjects and for an annual, week-long conference of Christian ecologists, with authoritative spokespersons from government, Christian ministry and scientific circles. For perhaps a dozen years or so, Au Sable has also published its findings and the text of lectures given at the Institute.

The environmental dimensions of the Christian mission

"Missionary earthkeeping" is one of the terms introduced into the ecological lexicon by Au Sable. The adjective has a double meaning—it refers to the expansive spirit of those who care for the earth. Most specifically, however, it speaks to the environmental dimensions of the Christian mission in the world—particularly in developing countries.

To many of the first category of "missionary" ecologists I feel a deep sense of obligation. The perceptive writings of Barry Commoner, Paul Ehrlich, Dennis Meadows, Lester Brown and others have illuminated my own environmental pilgrimage. But in the last decade, the earthkeeping missionaries have given me the most encouragement and balance and have helped me analyze my missionary task more biblically and scientifically.

Speaking as the "MK" ("Missionary's Kid") son of missionaries to Asia and as one who has spent most of his own life as a missionary in Latin America, I think I can state without fear of contradiction that most missionaries go overseas with plenty of their own cultural baggage, but with very little ecological perception.

Generally, spiritual values preoccupy us more than material ones. The gospel message is first in our priorities—protecting the environment is probably at the bottom of the list.

We take with us to the mission field only a fuzzy understanding of how the world works and how we as the human species relate to it. We feel little responsibility for the degradation of the environment and little motivation for stopping it. We have never tried in depth to understand what the Scriptures say about ecology and have never preached a sermon on the subject.

Those of us who are professional missionaries think of Christian stewardship more in terms of the use of money than of environmental protection. We have never really thought through our theology of nature and have not learned to apply what we know to our ethics and lifestyles. Most of us have also failed to appreciate the native environmental experience and insights in the areas where we have gone to minister in Jesus' name.

You may argue that other priorities concern the overseas missionary—such as evangelism, church planting, Christian education, or even the quality of the missionary's own devotional life and witness. That is true—and so it should be. But we are not dealing here so much with priorities of action and program as with perspectives and understanding of our task.

For example, why do we expect that someone wanting to be a church planter should study the whole gamut of theology? Why not just teach the church planter about church growth and turn him or her loose? Or why do we expect an evangelist-in-training to study church history? Or a Christian educator, ethics?

It is to ensure balance and completeness in the ministry. It is because the cumulative knowledge and experience in these related areas provide a safe platform from which to approach objectively one's own area of specialized research and ministry. It is a way to avoid bias, distortion and heresy. It helps preserve and communicate the full teaching of God's Word.

Accurate perspective is a matter of triangulation. If you can line up the sights of your transit from several well-established points, you can precisely identify and find your target. Ecological awareness is one of these important points and will help you from skewing your missionary perception of reality.

Recommended reading for missionaries

I would like to recommend four or five books that every Christian "missionary"—whether or not that missionary is serving overseas—should read. These books, most of them published within the last year, will give you what you need for triangulating reality for the twenty-first century.

1. Ghillean T. Prance & Calvin B. DeWitt, editors, *Missionary Earthkeeping* (Macon, Georgia: Mercer University Press, 1992). Contributors are J. Mark Thomas, Dennis E. Testerman, Robert Clobus, Mutombo Mpanya and James W. Gustafson. This book is Au Sable's latest contribution to Christian environmentalism.

2. Al Gore, *Earth in the Balance: Ecology and the Human Spirit* (New York: Houghton Mifflin Company, 1992). Already a durable best seller, this well-written book by the vice president of the United States is a text without peer. Everyone should read it.

3. Clive Ponting, *A Green History of the World: The Environment and the Collapse of Great Civilizations* (New York: St. Martin's Press, 1991). Most histories are the story of the victors. The perspective of the victims in this work is full of surprises.

4. Paul Harrison, *Inside the Third World* (Middlesex, England: Penguin Books, 1979, 1982, 1984). This book is not recent, but is a classic, linking poverty, climate and development in incontrovertible ways.

5. Loren Wilkinson, editor, *Earthkeeping in the Nineties: Stewardship of Creation* (Grand Rapids, Michigan: Eerdmans, 1980, 1991). For a complete theological treatment of stewardship and the environment, see the substantially revised 1991 version of this classic.

Having a healthy respect for other cultures

While a study of ecological principles would seem to be a requirement for every missionary candidate, there is probably just as much a missionary can learn on the "mission field" as in the "homeland." Major requisites are a humble spirit and a respect for the target culture.

Ghillean Prance, perhaps the world's leading authority on the ecology of the Amazon River basin, relates how the Chacobo Indians of Bolivia use nearly every available tree species for medicines, edible fruits, fuel and craft and building materials.[73]

Calvin DeWitt gives another example of a bushman who was able to identify by name 206 out of 211 collected plant varieties, and could draw finer distinctions between them than a trained botanist.

DeWitt also states that in the Filipino Hanunoo tribe, adults could identify 1,600 different species—some 400 more than previously recorded in a systematic botanical survey. "Often indigenous people are superior to scientists not only in knowledge of species," he comments, "but also in empirically understanding ecosystems."[74]

In the light of such "primitive" expertise, we cannot but recognize with botanist Prance "that the environmental impact of missions ranges from good to bad and, however good the intentions, mission work generally does not include adequate consideration or knowledge of environmental factors."[75]

This does not mean that we should overlook the evil in primitive societies—the fighting, raids, poisoning and the like. Prance himself points out that "the effort . . . is not to portray French philosopher Jean Jacques Rousseau's concept of the 'noble savage,' for all have sinned and come short of the glory of God."[76]

But lack of cross-cultural respect is not our only problem. As missionaries, we also appear to be ignorant of the scriptural doctrine and ethic of ecology. Our activities and perspective on the mission field have often paved the way for self-interested enterprise, thus contributing to the human arrogance, ignorance and greed that the Bible so strongly opposes.

We can see the environmental disorientation of many missions and missionaries in the medieval monks who cut down sacred trees to root out popular superstition. Or in an early twentieth century missionary to the Belgian Congo (Zaïre) who is reputed to have said, "I made up my mind that I would make it my work to bring the heathen out of the forest, to give them sunlight, to show them how to live in God's open world, to teach them to abandon this darkness . . . It was wonderful to see the forest coming down on all sides. I could feel the power of Satan receding as every tree fell."[77]

Outstanding examples of missionary earthkeepers

Despite these all-too-common attitudes, the history of Christian missions has also produced and is today producing many outstanding examples of missionary earthkeepers in the tradition of St. Francis of Assisi, who modeled humility and respect for God's creation.

In no particular order of priority, let me mention some who have been an encouragement to me. A few of them I count among my respected friends.

Unpredictable ground-breaker. William Carey, sometimes called the "father of modern missions," was more than a preacher-missiologist. He was also an amateur botanist. He founded the

Agricultural and Horticultural Society of India, was a member of the Linnaean Society, and a conservationist who understood and practiced missionary earthkeeping. In 1811 he made an unprecedented call for forest conservation, which has gone more or less unheeded.[78]

Medical missionary to Africa. Despite his earned doctorates in philosophy, theology, music and medicine, Dr. Albert Schweitzer was a humble man of God with a sincere reverence for all that God has created. "A man is ethical," he wrote, "only when Life, as such, is sacred to him, that of plants and animals as that of his fellow men; and devotes himself helpfully to all that is in need of help."[79]

Japanese poet. Part theologian and part mystic, Toyohiko Kagawa was also a lover of God's creation. He influenced Japanese land reform and mountain reforestation policies.

World-class statesman. No one has impacted the official, international world about environmental issues in a more powerful way than has Dr. Maurice Strong of Canada. Not a professional missionary, but an environmentalist of missionary mentality and long-time service in the YMCA, he organized the first UN conference on environment in Stockholm, Sweden, in 1972, was the founding director of the UNEP (United Nations Environmental Programme) in Nairobi, Kenya, and coordinated the Brazil Earth Summit in 1992.

Long ago, as a successful businessman, Strong recognized the importance of international cooperation and agreements for the protection of the earth's ecosphere. For the last twenty-some years, therefore, he has used his extraordinary talents of organization and persuasion to move the UN in earthkeeping directions.

Priest of God's handiwork. Formerly a Southern Baptist missionary to Japan, Luther Copeland elevates the Christian role in ecology above dominion and even stewardship. "We are stewards," he says, "but we are more than stewards . . . We are priests who view the world with reverence because it is God's handiwork. We are to represent the Creation to God and act toward it according to [God's] attitude and intent."[80]

102

Sage of Au Sable. As director and lecturer of the Au Sable Institute with its annual seminars and forums, Calvin DeWitt has become North America's most eloquent Christian spokesman of environmental insights. He is truly the godfather of missionary earthkeeping. His balance of Christian faith and scientific authority has given all of us a more solid foundation for our environmental convictions.

Holistic missionary. Serving with the Mission Covenant Church in Thailand, James Gustafson has successfully struggled to change spiritual values while seeking a "dynamic equivalent" as he puts the gospel to practice in local ecological situations. He has found that "the true value system of the gospel is constantly at loggerheads with the value systems of all societies."

Establishing a Center for Church Planting and Church Growth in northeast Thailand, together with the "Issan Development Foundation" to deal with the socioeconomic needs of the people, Gustafson's ministry has given birth to over 100 churches. It also has promoted the integration of social and spiritual ministry, including the development of local ecosystems or integrated farming systems. The aim is for new communities to grow in a "new relationship to God, humanity, and nature, and to develop a dynamic new lifestyle in response to God's grace."[81]

Intentional environmentalist. Dennis Testerman's friendship is also a source of encouragement for me. A candidate for foreign missionary service with the Southern Baptist board, Testerman expressed his desire to minister overseas in earth-saving ways, particularly in Pakistan.

The Baptist executives were wise enough and generous enough to recognize that they had no openings in Pakistan and encouraged Dennis to be seconded to the Presbyterian Church (U.S.A.). He followed their advice and for three years labored in mission posts in Nigeria and Pakistan that reflected his calling both as an evangelist and an environmentalist. He is now a resource conservation specialist in North Carolina.

Seed scatterer. Dr. Martin Price and his wife Bonnie were on their honeymoon in Costa Rica when I first met them. Martin was a professor at Purdue University, and an authority on sorghum. Yet he felt drawn to serve on the mission field or somehow to use his expertise to serve missionaries.

After much prayer and exploration, the Prices gave up academia for a life of faith. Bonnie got a job in Ft. Myers, Florida, and Martin set up a small experimental and seed farm just outside of town.

From that vantage point he has been able to build a network of missionary contacts around the world, to offer new varieties of seeds for providing food to near-famine areas, to accommodate graduate students on scholarship and to provide practical internships to furloughed missionaries.

Al Gore has suggested that the world's famines may often be famines not of food but of seeds, because existing varieties of grain have become vulnerable to pests and we have inadequate reserves of genes with which to engineer their renewed resistance.

Martin Price and his associates at ECHO (Educational Concerns for Hunger Organization) are helping many to keep the earth's food sources renewed and life-sustaining. His promotion of shallow roof-gardens has been particularly innovative for urban societies.

Eloquent roommate. Sharing my room at Au Sable in 1985 was a Catholic missioner from Ghana, Fr. Robert Clobus, a Dutch priest with poetic insights. I shall never forget his rationale for doing little things—seemingly inconsequential things—to care for the earth. He once said:

"I was at a loss as to what to do and where to begin, when I met a man who in his own small way makes little gardens in a desert world, and who is content with doing just that. He explained the power of the sign to me.

"When night is dark, and nothing can be seen, it is the spark of light which restores hope that a new day will break. When nobody sees a way out, and accepts a given situation as unchangeable, it is that one remark—that one refusal to accept or to admit defeat—which leads us on. When everybody says it can't be done, and someone does it—all those who seek have found.

"A sign is a bit like the Cross," Clobus said. "It is of necessity isolated, out of place—at once a sign of ridicule and a symbol of hope. By many it is misunderstood or dismissed as irrelevant. But some will recognize it as the beacon they have been looking for all their lives.

"It is given to man to assist God in creating such signs of hope. That is what I want to bring about—small gardens that will shine as green lights of hope in a land of yellow dryness. I want to prove to people that there is a way of living with God's earth—that it is possible to keep the earth, and treasure her, and make her flower and produce a hundredfold."[82]

These are just a few of the Christian ecologists who are standing in the front lines for us and have been an encouragement to me in my own path of environmental awareness.

If anyone ever decides to establish a Fraternity of Missionary Earthkeepers, I want to sign up with them as a charter member.

14
Countdown

No one can say for sure when the world will end. We have this on the best authority. Jesus himself said:

> . . . *no one knows the date and hour when the end will be—not even the angels. No, nor even God's Son. Only the Father knows. (Matt. 24:36)*

Of course, that has not kept many charlatans, cultists and false prophets from making a guess—always a mistaken one.

Yet, conversely, our Lord himself urges his followers to watch the signs of the times attentively in order to prepare for his return. In the same passage quoted above, Jesus says:

> *Now learn a lesson from the fig tree. When her branch is tender and the leaves begin to sprout, you know that summer is almost here. Just so, when you see all these things beginning to happen, you can know that my return is near, even at the doors. Then at last this age will come to its close. (Matt. 24:32-34)*

An accurate index of the "end times"

I believe that the most accurate index of the end times is the deterioration of the planetary ecosphere of which we are a part. In the spirit of Christ's exhortation in the Gospel of Matthew, I have been venturing some spot checks on the state of the earth—looking at some worrisome holes and threadbare spots, along with a few hopeful patches on God's environmental garment. The clearly discernible trends show clearly that we are frighteningly close to overload and breakdown.

Obviously, this is not the first attempt to see things in an objective way. At the end of the eighteenth century, Robert Malthus correctly observed that the growth of the earth's human population was multiplying geometrically and outpacing its potential for food production. He was mistaken in his time frames, but the analysis of trends was accurate.

Likewise, a computerized model of the biosphere, commissioned by the Club of Rome more than twenty years ago, attempted to trace the factors involved—population, atmospheric pollution, land use, water quantity and quality, impact of industry, transportation and agriculture, along with other significant trends such as the extinction of species and the loss of ozone. The projected results of this study showed the deterioration lines could conceivably cross the line of sustainability sometime between 2010 and 2040.[83]

Malthus underestimated the elasticity of the biosphere and the technical advance of society. The Club of Rome probably could not compute all the complex factors involved. But the declining trends they pointed out in each instance are undeniably accurate.

Another annual survey called *State of the World*, published by the Worldwatch Institute of Washington, D.C., does not attempt to be either comprehensive or prophetic in any one year or in any single published volume. It merely tries to report progress on the road to a sustainable society—but the net result continues to be discouraging.

It is virtually impossible, of course, to assess with precision all the worldwide factors involved in the ecosphere's sustainability of life—factors that are economic, agricultural, demographic, medical, industrial, biological, botanical, cultural and political. But we would be unfaithful stewards not to do the best we can.

We can almost tick off on the fingers of one hand the worst threats to human life—those most difficult to halt or reverse. The trends are measurable and definitely in decline. We can only hope they do not pick up too much speed, or exacerbate each other and trigger new threats.

First is human numbers and health

During 1970-1990 the world's population grew more than 40 percent—the equivalent of 1.6 billion people. In the next two decades experts expect it to grow even more, by 1.7 billion, bringing the total population to 7 billion.

Populations in developed countries are now growing by only half a percent a year. In developing countries, growth rates have fallen to slightly more than two percent a year. Some regions, including parts of Asia, Central America and the Caribbean, have reduced growth dramatically. Others, such as Africa (where growth has risen to three percent a year), have done less well.

Poverty is a major factor in the population explosion and infant mortality is one of the most tragic indicators of poverty. As mentioned in an earlier chapter, there are still 34 developing countries in which more than one in 10 children dies before he or she reaches the age of five. Few mothers opt for smaller families in the face of such risks. So—paradoxically—efforts to keep children alive and healthy are one of the keys to reducing population growth rates.[84]

Next comes water—measured both in quantity and quality

Shortages of drinkable water are increasingly common. The greatest demand for water is in industrialized nations that practice irrigation. Agriculture accounts for 69 percent, and industry for 23 percent of the water consumed on the planet. While there is a vast discrepancy in the amount of water used by different countries and cultures, domestic use accounts for only eight percent of the total.

According to GEMS (the United Nations Global Monitoring System), nitrate levels in the European rivers being measured are, on average, 45 times higher than in unpolluted rivers. Phosphates and pesticides also cause widespread pollution. This is not confined to industrialized countries—Colombia, Tanzania and Malaysia report similar findings.[85]

Sewage and agricultural nitrates contaminate marine foods and cause "red tides"—sometimes known as "dead zones." For example, Japan's Inland Sea, experiences about 200 such tides, mainly toxic, every year.[86]

The air we breathe is the third major threat

Excessive air pollution is greatest in developed nations and in urban areas. Mexico City, Tokyo, São Paulo and Los Angeles contend with it constantly. Air quality is by measurement unacceptable in 23 major cities in the world, and marginal in many others.[87] In the U.S., about 164 million Americans are at risk of respiratory and other problems, according to the American Lung Association.

In 1991, the Association found that 66 percent of the U.S. population lived in 534 counties and cities that violated federal clean air standards for ozone, carbon monoxide, lead and three other pollutants. At highest risk are the 31 million children and 19 million elderly Americans living in those areas. Their lungs are particularly sensitive to pollution.

The findings of the American Lung Association showed that the number of pollution-violating communities in the U.S. in only three years had increased almost 10 percent, and that the number of persons at risk had increased by 18 million, or 12 percent.[88]

The American experience is being repeated in other industrialized nations and developing urban centers.

The fourth imminent threat is to our land and trees

Wind and rain remove more than 25 billion tons of topsoil from farmland every year, besides that lost from other areas by natural erosion. In the U.S., 44 percent of cropland is affected by soil erosion; in El Salvador, 77 percent of all land is eroded; and farmers have had to abandon 38 percent of Nepal's fields because of land degradation.[89]

GLASOD (the Global Assessment of Land Degradation) suggests that human activities have degraded 15 percent of the earth's arable land. The mismanagement of the planet's forests and woodlands matches that of its croplands. Deforestation is estimated at 16.8 million hectares a year. The world may not be able to satisfy its demand for sawn wood in only 20 years' time.

Forests prevent soil erosion and are nature's principal means of water management. When the Himalayas were covered with trees, Bangladesh suffered a major flood about twice a century. One in every four years is now the average.

Trees also play an important role in stabilizing climate. Deforestation is responsible for one-quarter to one-third of the carbon dioxide added to the atmosphere, with the consequent threat of global warming.[90]

The fifth immediate danger is the number of species at risk

About one-quarter of the earth's species risks extinction within the next 30 years—usually because their habitats are being destroyed. In fact, we could logically include this threat to our environment in threat number four, above. This is because tropical deforestation at present rates could eliminate up to 15 percent of these species by 2020.

Commercial interest has put many species—from whales to elephants—at risk. The pollution of land, air and water by industry and agriculture has also reduced the numbers of many species.[91]

Although initially the Bush administration refused to sign the biodiversity treaty brokered by the UNEP in Brazil in 1992, the Clinton administration has since endorsed the treaty. With U.S. backing, the move to slow the reduction of biodiversity may gain strength.

Industry, energy and waste are our sixth imminent threat

Industry produces environmental problems everywhere. It consumes 37 percent of the world's energy, and emits 50 percent of the world's carbon dioxide, 90 percent of the world's sulfur oxides and nearly all the toxic chemicals now threatening the ozone layer with depletion.

Every year industry produces 2.1 billion tons of solid waste and 338 million tons of hazardous waste. In developing countries, small scale, unregulated industries often discharge untreated waste.[92]

This litany of ecological trends could continue—to include excessive use of energy, damaging dependence on fossil-based fuels for transport and destruction of the earth's protective ozone layer and climatic equilibrium. Some trends are accelerating; some are being moderated; all of them are moving towards overload and arrest.

But allow me here to summarize by shifting metaphors.

A visit to Ms. Planet Earth

I would like for you to come with me to visit an elderly patient in the nursing home of a retirement community. It's a pleasant place, attractively decorated, with spacious corridors and comfortable lounges.

As we walk down the hall, we come to a door that is slightly ajar. On it, a small, neat placard reads "MS. PLANET EARTH."

Just as we are about to knock, out steps the doctor. He is a cheerful, good looking man in a white jacket, with his stethoscope dangling around his neck.

"Good morning," he says. "Are you here to visit Mother Earth?"

"Yes," we answer. "How is she?"

"Well, I'm glad to see your concern for her health. So many people don't seem to care what happens to her or how she is doing. Why don't you slip into the lounge with me for a minute and let me tell you about her?"

We step into the nearby waiting room and make ourselves comfortable in a cluster of overstuffed chairs.

"I'm sure I don't need to remind you," the doctor says to us, "that this patient is mortal. She's going to have to die sooner or later. . . . No, no, no, no . . ." He lifts his hand to signal STOP when we try to interrupt him.

"I understand that none of us want to see her go. And she's a tough old lady! When I say she's mortal, I don't mean she's dying today. I just mean that we cannot reasonably anticipate full recovery. That's where we have to start in our assessment of her condition.

"She is, after all, quite elderly. She's lived a long and productive life. Even now, she still possesses amazing strength and resistance, and she's still beautiful, as you will discover when you see her." Almost in a whisper, the doctor adds, "She must have been really gorgeous in her youth! . . .

"What I mean by this," he goes on, "is that the medical treatment Mother Earth needs is aimed at survival, pain relief and maximum quality of life, instead of at full recovery. This makes a big difference in how we prescribe for her. We sometimes have to make tradeoffs—like allowing a certain amount of contamination in order not to eliminate altogether the nutritive elements in her diet."

Again we interrupt the doctor. "Can you give us any kind of prognosis—other than that we should be prepared for the worst?"

"It's not easy," the doctor replies. "Perhaps the best way to do it is to run down the list of her symptoms with you and let you draw your own conclusions. You have to understand that any one of them could suddenly become fatal—or a combination of two or more of them might affect her in ways we can't anticipate, and produce a terminal condition quite suddenly. The symptoms are all serious, and we need to treat them vigorously—which again is sometimes not so easy as it sounds."

Planet Earth's serious symptoms

At this point, the long years spent by the doctor in the classroom take over, and he moves to a flip chart and picks up a blue marker. "I'll try to list them," he says.

"1. First, she has trouble breathing. The air is polluted. This started way back when people learned to use fire, but anthropogenic air pollution has increased fantastically with industrialization and modern transportation. Mother Earth could very easily be done in by photochemical smog.

"2. Her temperature is going up. Excessive carbon dioxide and other chemicals produce what is called the 'greenhouse effect,' which could ultimately melt the planet's ice caps and raise the sea levels. Gaps in the ozone layer, volcanic eruptions and massive deforestation also affect her climate.

"3. The earth's inland water sources, as well as her oceans, are suffering from massive pollution. In many places potable water is excruciatingly scarce. Elsewhere, toxic wastes caused by industrial and agricultural chemicals, oil spills and sewage disposal have contaminated fisheries and recreational areas. These constitute a high risk to her health.

"4. Even looking superficially at Mother Earth reveals how scarce and abused is her land surface. Erosion, desertification, salinization, construction are all affecting her health. Too much chemical fertilizer and insecticides, in particular, have taken their toll.

"5. Closely related to the last two symptoms is the decimation of forests—particularly tropical rain forests—and coral reefs. These are the centers of biodiversity which normally teem with life and renew Mother Earth's energies. Now they are withered.

"6. We have already mentioned waste, I think. But I need to emphasize again that it is impossibly excessive. Traveling garbage—barges, trains and trucks—is common. This glut could easily prove fatal.

"7. Species are becoming extinct and oceans are being over-fished before you can snap your fingers! Of Mother Earth's original species, only one percent are still alive today. No wonder she is flat on her back, without energy.

"8. All of these symptoms make it very clear that she is basically overpopulated. She has never had to cope with such massive numbers of inhabitants

before, and it has laid her out. Her frame is carry-
ing ten times the weight she carried just a few
years ago! And it hasn't stopped growing! Obesity
is perhaps the most imminent threat to her life.

"9. I guess the most worrisome symptom of all is that
she is being so neglected. Nobody seems to be
aware of her condition. No one shows concern for
relieving her symptoms. We could do so much to
alleviate the situation, to reduce her pain and suffering, but there are so few who are interested in
getting involved."

The doctor lays down his marker and moves back to his
chair with a sigh.

"There are other dangerous symptoms that I could mention.
But these should be enough to show the seriousness of her condition."

We thank the doctor and rise to our feet, deep in thought.

"You may go in and see the patient now," he tells us. "I
know my prognosis has been very vague and unsatisfactory to you.
But please do what you can to make her final days as happy and
productive as possible."

We begin to move toward Mother Earth's room, but the
doctor's voice stops us.

"One final word. I have left an important factor out of my
report," he says. "My experience has taught me that human expertise is not always exact in cases like this one. In the last analysis, it
is God who holds all of us in his hands. He gives life, he takes it. He
can shorten it, he can prolong it. He can cure a disease or let it take
its course.

"I have tried to give you the facts as I see them. To me, it
looks like the end is not too far away. But I don't pretend to give
you God's will, nor to predict his timing. We can—and we all do—
pray for his mercy and restoration."

We thank the doctor again and enter the room quietly, so as
not to disturb the patient. She is seated in an armchair by the open

French doors, gazing wistfully at the manicured beauty of her small, flowered patio outside, and at the bare, brown mountains beyond her nursing home wall.

PART III - REACTIONS

Pressure Points in the Christian Mission

15
Walking lightly on the earth

Dwayne Hodgson and Ronald Sider

An American-style "green consumerism"—with its often half-hearted practice of the three Rs: REDUCE, REUSE and RECYCLE—is not enough for the faithful Christian.

The prophetic biblical vision of *shalom* demands that we move beyond the American norm to an obedient and joyful living that will protect creation and foster social justice. To do this we need to review our application of the three Rs, and indeed, to adopt three more Rs: REPENT, RETHINK and REJOICE!

There are many things that we can do to fulfill the biblical calling to live as faithful stewards of God's creation. The good news for Christians is that ecologically responsible living actually reinforces our efforts to promote social justice. These issues are clearly interdependent in both the biblical concept of *shalom* and in the contemporary problems that we face. A basic reorientation of our lifestyle, therefore, can help us to fulfill our responsibilities both to the poor and to the environment.

The purpose of this chapter is not to provide an exhaustive list of suggestions. Many other authors have already done an excellent job of this. Instead, it is to provide basic guidelines for making lifestyle choices.

A call to stewardship and redemptive living

Our starting point must be with the biblical mandate for environmental protection.

The environmental crisis has forced us to reevaluate our performance as "stewards" of God's creation. Too often we have misunderstood stewardship as "ownership," and we have tried to appropriate God's creation for our selfish, shortsighted, and often destructive purposes.[93] As servants made in the "image of God" (Gen. 1:27, NIV), however, we must be obedient in "[upholding] God's intended purpose for creation" by protecting and tending it.[94]

Ecologically sound living also reflects Christ's redemption of creation. The Bible clearly teaches that salvation means not only the redemption and resurrection of Christians, but also that "the creation itself will be set free from its bondage to decay" (Rom. 8:21, RSV).[95] Although final salvation comes from God, we should "participate with him in caring for all parts of his creation, making our contribution to the work which he will complete on the day of his coming."[96]

Shalom: Justice and ecological harmony

Social justice and environmental protection are clearly related, both in the Bible and in our contemporary situation.

In the Old Testament, the concept of *shalom* or "peace" combines the liberation of the oppressed with the restoration of God's creation.[97] As Wesley Granberg-Michaelson writes:

> Injustice has its roots in seizing and controlling part of creation for one's own selfish desires and thereby depriving others of creation's fruits, making them poor, dispossessed and oppressed."[98]

Thus, those who oppress the poor disrupt *shalom* and violate the wholeness of God's creation. In contrast, the coming kingdom will mark the reconciliation of all creation (Col. 1:15-20) and the establishment of justice.[99]

The link between injustice and defiled creation is painfully evident today. The exorbitant lifestyle of the "First World," with our mass consumerism, fossil fuel addiction and insatiable appetite for more things, harms the poor and simultaneously creates environmental degradation on an unprecedented scale. For example, although we are only one-quarter of the global population, we produce 70 percent of all greenhouse gases. The resulting global warming could lead to dramatic climate changes, affecting other parts of the world, with mass starvation and rising sea levels.[100]

In many developing countries, inequitable land distribution, poverty-influenced population growth, and an emphasis on growing cash crops for export to the North forces poor farmers to grow crops on marginal lands or erosion-prone hillsides, or to slash-and-burn tropical rain forests as a means of survival.[101]

Clearly the plight of the poor is tied inexorably to the excess of the wealthy, and we share a common danger in the environmental crisis. As Christians, we must respond.[102]

Repentance: The first "R"

If our present situation is a product of sin, the first "R" that Christians must practice is clearly **repentance**.

Our current economic patterns are obviously incompatible with reducing global poverty and preserving a livable planet for future generations.[103] What's more, our assumption of an irresponsible mastery over creation amounts to sin, both through our personal choices that destroy *shalom*, and our voluntary and involuntary participation in structural evils that denigrate the environment and oppress the poor.[104]

The problem is fundamentally spiritual in nature. So the "enlightened self-interest" of much of secular environmental ethics is insufficient to address the true roots of environmental decay.[105] What we need is biblical repentance: the recognition of guilt, the acceptance of forgiveness, and conscious conversion or "turning around" to new ways of living.[106]

Christian repentance provides hope for real change because it is through the redemptive power of Christ, says Tony Campolo, that we can "find the strength to exercise the kind of self-control that the world needs."[107] In Christ, he continues, "we will be able to escape the bondage of the culturally prescribed, consumeristic lifestyle that has brought us to the brink of environmental disaster."[108] Through Christ we can struggle against the demonic "principalities and powers" that underlie the destruction of nature, and we can build *shalom.*[109]

Rethink: Getting to the root cause

While repentance is crucial, clearly we must fundamentally **rethink** our patterns of living in order to address the underlying problems. Environmental destruction goes far beyond our choice of diapers at the supermarket.

We can link many of our environmental woes to the fundamental assumptions that underlie North American culture: our unabashed materialism and consumerism; our uncritical belief that progress, efficiency and technological fixes will correct all our problems; our excessive individualism that prevents economic sharing and places competition above community; our physical and emotional distance from the land and nature; and the predominance of economic criteria that precludes making sustainable and moral choices if they are considered remotely "uneconomic."[110]

These assumptions are so fundamental that we don't even give them much thought.[111] If we are to act as agents of redemption for creation, however, we need to appraise critically how we apply them.

The issue of "green consumerism" provides a good example. While choosing "environmentally friendly" products is important, we still base this on the materialistic assumption that we have the right to more things—just as long as they are "green"—and that we can infinitely increase our consumption despite the limits of a finite environment. What's more, many "environmentally friendly" products remain more expensive than their "unfriendly" equivalents. This may reflect real costs or outright profiteering, but practically it means that green consumerism becomes the prerogative of the wealthy, the hallmark of the "enviro-yuppie" lifestyle.[112]

Admittedly, it is easy to criticize the philosophical foundations of our society. It is much more difficult to live in ways that run contrary to the prevailing flow.[113]

As Dorothy Jansen Longacre suggests in her book, *Living More With Less*, we can best meet this challenge in some form of Christian community. For some, this is found in "intentional communities" where people share resources and live communally. For others, it may lie with the mutual accountability of a Bible study group where members support each other in their simple lifestyle choices. Or it may start with a shared, congregational "tool closet of common household and garden tools."[114] Again, the point is not to legislate us all into "environmental Pharisees," but to encourage us to simple, yet infinitely richer and more creative modes of living.

Reducing: The neglected "R"

While there has been much talk about the three Rs, most of our attention seems to have focused on recycling, and very little has been said about **reducing** our consumption. Recycling is certainly an important step, but it often amounts to no more than throwing our garbage into a different-colored box—it doesn't really challenge our addiction to materialism.

Certainly we should buy "green" to encourage more environmentally benign and socially just manufacturing, trade and agricultural practices. But environmentalism for Christians must be more than just a shopping list of choices. We need to reconsider the list itself.

We need to judge our standard of living in terms of a right relationship with God, people, and the earth. We need to learn to be content with meeting our basic material needs, to reconsider the "wants" that society claims we "need," and to find joy in nonmaterial, creative alternatives.[115] We need to step outside the rat race and avoid competitive comparisons that make us continually dissatisfied with what we have.

In pursuing a simple lifestyle, we can free resources that can meet the needs of the poor in our communities and around the world. By nonconforming freely we can promote justice, nurture community and "choose to fit the way we live to the environment," instead of "trying to reshape the environment to our whims."[116]

Reuse: Sustainable living

Although many people now recognize that the disposable ethic of the 1970s was environmentally disastrous, it is surprising how this attitude persists. Excess packaging is a good example. Although related to our insistence on convenient, immaculately clean and risk-free products, as well as to the requirements of retail marketing, most packaging becomes "instant garbage" once we step outside the store. The constant change in clothing styles is another example, as people will replace perfectly useful clothes to keep up with the latest fad.

As environmentally concerned Christians, we need to learn to **Reuse**. We should reconsider the hectic pace of our lives that requires the use of convenience products. We need to use items that are reusable (e.g., rechargeable batteries) and durable. When possible, we should buy what we need in bulk or with the least among of packaging. We must cut back on our use of non-renewable resources like fossil fuels, and rely more on renewable alternatives.[117]

When we need to purchase things, we should use "full-cycle costing" and consider the larger environmental, social and economic impacts of the manufacturing, sale, use and disposal of the product. We should learn to buck the latest trends and be content with less fashionable clothes and furniture.

These measures are more than a knee-jerk, anti-consumerism stance—they are part of a conscious decision about where we will store our riches, and consequently our hearts (Matt. 6:21).

Recycle: Completing the cycle

With the growing awareness of recycling programs in North America, we don't need to say more about this "R." If your community does not have a recycling program, then lobby for one. Or better yet, start one yourself through your school, office or church and let the politicians catch up with you![118]

We should continually expand recycling programs beyond cans, bottles and newspapers to include fine paper, plastics (both PVC and PET), cardboard, grocery bags, used car oil and batteries.[119]

We must also make a conscious decision to complete the cycle by buying recycled products ourselves. One of the largest snags in recycling has been the glut in used materials that lie unused in warehouses. Unless we insist on using recycled products, there is no economic incentive for firms to use recycled materials.[120]

Rejoice—God so loves this world!

The final "R" that we must practice as Christians is to **rejoice!** Too often we can get bogged down in a pharisaic list of do's and don'ts, and we can lose sight of whom we are serving through our alternative lifestyle. We need to remember that we are acting as servants to our Lord in walking lightly on the earth, and to remember that despite the growing tide of environmental degradation, it is God's design to restore creation (Rom. 8).

We need to rejoice in finding new ways of living creatively , ways that produce community, justice and ecological harmony—things that our society has lost in the pursuit of materialism.

Finally, we need to rejoice in the gift of God's creation and God's continual provision for the world (Ps. 104). We should take time to break out of the suburbs and the rat race, to take a hike in a park or wilderness area, to appreciate the created order that lives right in our inner cities. We should join with nature in the worship of our Maker, Sustainer and Redeemer. As Campolo writes:

> Feel the ecstasy of all the things that you can smell and touch and hear in this too-often-taken-for-granted world. Taste and see that the Lord is good (Psalm 34:8). And learn to be thrilled with the extraordinary ordinary things that are all around you.[121]

Conclusion: It's only the start!

While setting your own house in order is the logical place to start, it is only a beginning. If we limit our environmental action to personal lifestyle choices, we only fall into the individualistic mindset of Western culture, and the perception that our power is limited to token votes in the "democracy of the marketplace."

True environmental change requires a much broader revision of social values and actions, and as Christians we must be vocal in our social and political activism to protect and sustain creation.

16

Patching garments . . . patching communities

Stephen K. Commins

Nepal is a highly mountainous, ecologically fragile country. Over the past several decades, soil loss by erosion on farms has increased. This means that people are poorer and more desperate.

When you visit Nepal, you find people moving out of rural areas. This is a sign that farming systems are falling apart. Soil loss is a severe problem in many communities, but at first there appears to be little one can do to stop this problem.

The Jajarkot district is typical of the middle hill areas of Nepal, lying between the plains and the mountains. The cutting down of forests has occurred rapidly over the past forty years as an increasing population widens its search for firewood, timber and land to cultivate.

Soil now under cultivation is typically lacking in organic material and of poor structure. When rainfall is irregular, crops fail disastrously. Malnutrition is widespread, and essential nutrients are lacking because of the monotony of the diet.

Signs of hope in a problem area

Underneath the big problem, however, one finds small patchwork signs of hope.

127

At one farm, a walk through the fields shows a gentle approach to soil and farm regeneration. Closest to the house is the vegetable garden, where beans, peas, cucumbers, tomatoes, mint, cauliflower, cabbage and many other vegetables and herbs are grown together. Continuous ground cover, vegetables in various stages of maturity, or mulch suppress the growth of weeds.

Strategic placement of plants helps realize their full benefits. Garlic and onion are mixed with brassicas and potatoes, making use of the former's pest-repellent properties. Similarly, marigolds—whose flowers the Nepalese use for ceremonial purposes—are interplanted with tomatoes to attract hoverflies, whose larvae eat the tomato whitefly. The leguminous "ipil ipil" (leucaena) tree is planted throughout the garden. This tree, besides fixing nitrogen and producing leaves that make excellent fodder and mulch, provides protection from the sun and wind and support for climbing beans and cucumber plants. There is an emphasis on perennials throughout the farm.

At a second farm, an hour's walk away in the valley bottom, rice is grown using the no-tillage method based on the Fukuoka system, developed in Japan. The basic method of using permanent living mulch of clover to fix nitrogen, keep down weeds and retain moisture seems to be working well. Arable crops are also being grown, using traditional methods, supplemented by green manures.

Why has the project been such a success? And what can we learn from it? As a development method it is obvious, as one observer has commented, that "villages have to see and believe permaculture in action before they can be expected to accept it themselves." And indeed, the demonstration farms can be seen from miles away, standing out as fertile oases against the degraded landscape.[122]

But more fundamentally, it is evident that "patching God's garment" is a matter of hard work, as well as of new vision.

The burden of earthkeeping, which reflects our reverence for God's creation, often calls for laborious exertion in small ways. This is particularly true in poor countries, where the regeneration of the earth is so important. Poverty and ecological destruction are closely linked, and human well-being depends on environmental renewal.

The metaphor of "patching" is particularly appropriate for looking at how people live in poor communities. This is because the poor are always struggling to keep their "garment"—their soil and resources, their ecosystem, as well as their clothes—from wearing out by applying patches to strategic, threadbare spots.

"Patching" and sustainable development

Another term closely linked to the vision of patching is that of "sustainable development." The ideal of sustainability is rooted in environmental concerns. It is based on the belief that current economic—and particularly, agricultural—practices cannot sustain or regenerate the earth's resources for future generations. Hence, they need to be modified, or "patched."

Until recently, experts have traditionally based development on an acceptance of economic growth as the essential hallmark of progress. During the past two decades, however, it has become apparent that the predominant development models—in both developed and developing countries—are in conflict with the earth's ecological realities.

The emphasis on satisfying economic and social needs through unchecked growth is no longer acceptable, especially when a significant portion of the population lacks even the basics for adequate human welfare.

And most importantly, we can no longer consider the destruction of the earth's natural resource base as a necessary tradeoff for improved living conditions.

One of the greatest obstacles to encouraging sustainable development practices is rooted in how outside organizations relate to low income communities. Development—which must take into account the protecting and regenerating of natural resources—cannot succeed without first involving the people of those very communities that have the greatest need. These communities cannot afford development programs that undermine their long-term ability to survive.

Nor can there be success if the priorities of international agencies take precedence over those of local people. The immediate needs and problems of poor communities should be the central concern of every development organization. Community members are more likely to be able to identify their needs. There is an inevitable gap between how outsiders perceive the needs of a local community and how the community members themselves define them.

Understanding sustainable development through "SLT"

One way of understanding sustainable development is through "SLT." Sustainable livelihood thinking (SLT) has emerged as one approach for reversing the relationship between outsiders and local people.

Robert Chambers developed the concept of SLT, based on his extensive experience in Africa and Asia. He has written widely on new approaches to development practice.[123] At the root of the SLT concept is the idea that the perceptions and priorities of low-income people can provide the basis for the establishment and direction of sustainable development programs.

"Sustainable" refers to the ability to protect or regenerate the resource base available to low-income people. People can design practices and programs that improve a household's economic well-being—or that of a community—to enhance and not merely exploit the environment.

"Livelihood" means that people have adequate access to food or cash, as well as some reserves (such as animals, trees, marketable products) that can help them meet their basic needs. This kind of security can come from a variety of sources, including legal land tenure, livestock and forests, stable employment, or a combination of the above. The key to a secure livelihood is the existence of protection or buffers against disasters such as crop failures or illness to adults in the family.

Approaching development work from the perspective of SLT offers obvious advantages to low-income communities. Poor people would be better equipped to survive in difficult seasons.

The resources of the community would be managed in a more enduring manner, with more decision-making in the hands of those most directly affected by the programs. As a result, there would be less outmigration to cities because poverty would be reduced, thus providing more economic and social stability within the community and less pressure on already overcrowded urban areas. It is likely that the communities would also have lower population growth rates, as families experience a greater sense of economic protection and security.

To achieve this, development at the local level must incorporate low-income people's definition of their own needs and problems. So "thinking" in SLT refers to understanding people's perceptions of their own lives and well-being, and using those insights to guide development planning.

Chambers argues that people will achieve sustainable development only when development is practiced from the perspective of the poor, and not of the "experts." He quotes a remark that ". . . for every problem there is a solution that is simple, direct and wrong." He goes on to say:

> Simple, direct solutions which tried to solve problems of population growth directly and only by family planning, of resource depletion directly and only by controls, of environmental degradation directly and only by conservation, and of development directly and only by growth—all had some validity, but all were unsubtle, with neglected linkages, and generally did not work well. These simple, direct solutions shared the weakness of starting with physical problems only and not social relations, and often with the concerns and values of the rich rather than those of the poor.[124]

Community patching work in the SLT mode has strong parallels to a servant-based approach in development. It is aware of complexity, yet is simple in building relationships. It builds on the local knowledge within a community. It involves people, and it respects the limits of the environment.

SLT is part of a learning mindset. For Christians, it means a humility towards God and towards neighbor. Patching is part of acknowledging the Creator's gifts, working as servants, not as masters of creation.

Signposts of success

People have described the Sahel belt of West Africa as the "border of hell." In this apocalyptic setting, over a number of years, Lutheran World Relief established a program for building wells in a number of villages. The wells were dug with local labor and mostly local materials.

Farmers began work with simple hand buckets that carried water from the wells to gardens that bloomed quickly in the hot climate. Over the years, they planted larger gardens using gravity irrigation—allowing the water to run down from a well dug at a slightly higher elevation.

During a particularly dry year in the late 1980s, community workers found that these gardens were the source of security for local farmers.

Omosheleko, Ethiopia, is another signpost of success. Peter Cormack of World Vision wrote of the task of seeing enduring balances there.[125] Work began by asking farmers how they protected the land, how they maintained soil fertility and how they prevented erosion. The farmers created bunds (ditches dug on the contour of the land) to catch water run-off and prevent erosion. They feared being drawn into the cost trap of expensive fertilizers. But it was hard to know what else to do.

The program in Omosheleko involved working with those who wanted to use risk-reducing approaches that were less dependent on outside resources. By using a mixture of crops in the same field, farmers reduced the chances of cropless seasons. They mixed such plants as corn, squash and beans in the same field, which also lessens the need for purchasing fertilizers.

Over the years, those trying to "help" farmers with modern, costly technologies have made many mistakes. This did not involve patching—it involved running over the learning of past generations. Now, different attitudes are emerging—attitudes that think about sustainable livelihoods.

Indispensable dimensions of development

John Steward of World Vision Australia has identified several key issues for people involved in community development work. We can call these issues indispensable dimensions of development. They include such subjective factors as team unity, reflection, evaluation and flexibility as prerequisites for success. As might be expected, ownership of objectives, control of activities and income generation are basic developmental elements. But so are education, recognition of environmental limits and world view paradigms.[126] Altogether, development is not so simple as it once seemed to be!

Patching God's garment—having an SLT mindset—challenges outsiders to appreciate the capacity and knowledge of low-income people. It connects sustainable development as a general concept to the particular situation of a specific community. This approach gives voice to those who are rarely heard in the circles of power, and allows us to understand development from new perspectives. Sustainable development is a matter of reversals in thought, reversals in action and reversals in relationships.

Hearing, seeing and learning about how the world looks from the bottom up, instead of from the top down, is a good way to live as servants and stewards of God's creation.

17

Global justice and the environment

Job S. Ebenezer

The alternatives are grim.

"If current predictions of population growth prove accurate and patterns of human activity on the planet remain unchanged, science and technology may not be able to prevent either irreversible degradation of the environment or continued poverty for much of the world." Thus reads a 1992 report from the U.S. National Academy of Sciences and the Royal Society of London.

Today one can sense desperation and hopelessness in the voices of environmentalists. Denis Hays, the organizer of the first Earth Day in 1970, said during the 1990 Earth Day celebrations, "Twenty years after the first Earth Day, those of us who set out to change the world are poised on the threshold of utter failure. Measured on virtually any scale, the world is in worse shape than it was 20 years ago. How could we who have fought so hard, and won so many battles, now find ourselves on the verge of losing the war?"

What can the church offer?

In the midst of this atmosphere of pessimism and hopelessness, what can the Christian church offer? Primarily, the church should proclaim boldly that environmental degradation and continued poverty are consequences of injustice. Unless we address the systemic causes of injustice, no amount of science and technology, public policy changes and environmental stewardship will restore God's creation to the sustainable state God intended.

The prophets recognized the link between injustice and environmental degradation long ago. The prophet Hosea wrote, ". . . there is no faithfulness, no kindness, no knowledge of God in your land. You swear and lie and kill and steal and commit adultery. There is violence everywhere, with one murder after another. That is why your land is not producing; it is filled with sadness, and all living things grow sick and die; the animals, the birds, and even the fish begin to disappear" (Hos. 4:1-3).

The prophet Jeremiah reflects God's anger in the following statement: "I brought you into a fertile land to eat its fruit and rich produce. But you came and defiled my land and made my inheritance detestable" (Jer. 2:7, NIV)

We hear similar cries in the prophecies of Ezekiel: "Must my flock feed on what you have trampled and drink what you have muddied with your feet?" (Ezek. 34:19, NIV)

These prophetic words clearly show that the justice spoken of in the Bible is not just for the poor, the widows, the orphans and the imprisoned, but also for the beasts, the birds, the fish and the land. God's justice encompasses both humankind and nature. Injustice done to many people results in injustice to God's creation, and vice versa.

The global economic system

What are some examples of unjust systems that cause environmental degradation?

The global economic system is a primary cause of environmental degradation and the increase in poverty. The industrialized and technologically advanced countries have an upper hand in today's economic practices. We know that the promotion of inexpensive exports from poor countries plunders the natural resources of those countries.

Take for example the production and export of so-called "nontraditional exports": fruits and vegetables grown in Latin America, Africa and Asia for export to North America, the former USSR and its allies and European countries. To produce insect-free and blemish-free products, poor farmers must spray toxic chemicals without benefit of protective clothing or masks. Many of these farmers not only lose their health but also their land to the high cost of inputs to practice modern agriculture. To supplement their income, they cut down trees for firewood and cause deforestation, mud slides and soil erosion.

Institutions in the industrialized countries fix the prices of nontraditional exports. This uncertainty forces many farmers to increase production with no concern for the well-being of the land. They do not rotate their crops nor do they provide rest for the land.

We read in Leviticus, "When you come into the land I am going to give you, you must let the land rest before the Lord every seventh year" (Lev. 25:2). The Bible contains many more instructions regarding a just economic system that treats both the poor and God's creation fairly. A thorough treatment of economic justice based on Scripture is found in Ronald J. Sider's book, *Rich Christians in an Age of Hunger*, published by Word Publishing Company.

Global debt

Global debt is another injustice affecting both the poor and the environment. The debt crisis has plagued developing countries since the 1980s.

One of the devastating consequences of the crisis is debt-induced resource exploitation. To service the debt, poor countries have resorted to an exploitation of natural resources in a less-than-sustainable manner. Clear-cutting of forests to export wood for paper and for building construction results in the loss not only of trees but also of biodiversity. Over-exploitation of oceans and lakes for seafood export is another example of how unjust debt servicing destroys aquatic biodiversity.

According to Christ, forgiveness of debts is a sign of the coming of the kingdom of God. Jesus emphasized forgiveness of debts in the parable of the king who settled accounts with his servants (Matt. 18:23-34). In the Lord's Prayer, Christ instructed us to pray: "Forgive us our debts, as we also have forgiven our debtors" (Matt. 6:12, NIV). Christians, whose moral stance is grounded in biblical ethics, should join with others who are trying to find just and equitable solutions to this injustice.

The North's affluent lifestyle

The affluent lifestyle of the North is yet another major cause of environmental degradation and poverty. Studies estimate that an affluent 20 percent of the population consumes about 80 percent of the world's resources. To satisfy the appetite of the affluent and provide them with cheap food and other consumer goods, women and children become victims of cheap labor and the environment of poor nations is degraded as well.

Besides depleting resources, affluent lifestyles also generate enormous amounts of waste. The lax rules and regulations regarding the safety of workplaces and the handling and disposing of hazardous wastes compromise both human and environmental health.

Some multinational corporations transport hazardous waste large distances for disposal in poor neighborhoods of our own country and in poor countries abroad. Some Western nations export hazardous waste for disposal in poor countries without alerting those who live nearby about the nature of the waste and its threat to human health.

Both the Old and New Testaments teach us that we must care for and protect the poor when the rich exploit them. Jesus's first public utterance was, "The Spirit of the Lord is upon me; he has appointed me to preach Good News to the poor . . ." (Luke 4:18). Christ warns the rich with these words, ". . . It is almost impossible for a rich man to get into the Kingdom of Heaven. I say it again—it is easier for a camel to go through the eye of a needle than for a rich man to enter the Kingdom of God" (Matt. 19:23-24)!

Reflecting the God we know and serve

An effective way for Christians to communicate Christ's gospel to the world in the next century may be through the practice of responsible lifestyles. If most of the Christians in affluent countries assess their effects on both the environment and the poor and make modest adjustments in their lifestyles, they can considerably reduce environmental degradation and the exploitation of the poor.

There are other global injustices that contribute to the degradation of God's creation and the oppression of the poor. Christians should address technology transfer, just compensation to native peoples for the use of medicinal plants from their forests, appropriate payments for safe waste disposal, and a host of other justice issues in the light of the Scriptures.

We worship a God of justice (Isa. 30:18, NIV), a God who loves justice and delights in it (Isa. 61:8 and Jer. 9:24, NIV). The prophet Micah calls us ". . . to be fair and just and merciful, and to walk humbly with your God" (Mic. 6:8). In Deuteronomy 16:19-20 (NIV), Moses reminded the Israelites: "Do not pervert justice or show partiality . . . Follow justice and justice alone, so that you may live and possess the land the Lord your God is giving you."

May our treatment of creation and the powerless in society reflect the God of justice revealed in the Law, in the prophets, and by Christ our Lord.

18

Training missionary earthkeepers

William A. Dyrness

Not too many years ago *missionary* and *ecology*, or even *pastor* and *ecologist*, would not have been mentioned in the same breath. Christians may even have thought of a *missionary ecology* as an oxymoron, a seeming contradiction.

Not that missionaries were unaware of the degradation of creation. Indeed they were often the first to see the reality of slash-and-burn farming, or the desertification brought on by drought and famine. But they, and the people they ministered to, seemed to have more urgent matters to attend to—or at least, matters they thought to be more urgent at the time.

Missiology and ecological concerns

I well remember the great clouds of black smoke pouring from the ancient buses I rode to work each morning in Manila during the 1970s. The brown haze now becoming common in American cities had long been the lot of Third World cities like Manila. I remember thinking that care for the environment was a luxury these people could not afford. They were struggling to feed and house their families. They did not have the time to "clean up" their city.

Indeed, the vast sums of money that Imelda Marcos spent on cleaning crews for the inner city filled us with righteous indignation: How could she divert this money from the urgent needs of the poor? Meanwhile, we missionaries had what to us was the irreplaceable task of helping people hear and receive the gospel. Somehow care for the earth did not seem to be a priority.

So when we taught our courses at the Asian Theological Seminary in the 1970s, we struggled to see the relevance of Scripture and church history for issues of poverty and injustice, but we gave no attention to ecological concerns.

Dayton Roberts has reminded us that if it ever was possible for missionaries to slight these concerns, it is becoming increasingly difficult for them to do so today. Twenty years ago we may have had the luxury of concluding that we could put off environmental problems, however serious they might be, for another day. Now, as this book points out, creation's cries of pain press us to respond urgently. Then it might have been understandable for a mission like ours to instruct all its missionaries to avoid all social and political activities in Third World countries and concentrate on the work of teaching and preaching the Bible. Today such a request is tantamount to urging us to abdicate our responsibilities as stewards of the gospel.

All of this has become increasingly clear to those who, like the author of this study, have taken the time to reflect on the issues. But what has been the response in terms of theological and missiological education? Has the urgency of our situation had any noticeable impact on the practice of training pastors and missionaries?

In our brief discussion of this question we will notice that while some significant theological reflection is taking place on the environment and its place in Christian theology, this reflection has not yet had any appreciable influence on curricula and programs.

Let us take up the second part of this claim first.

Are environmental questions peripheral to theological education?

It is clear from even a cursory examination of seminary curricula that Christian educators still consider environmental questions as peripheral to theological education. As far as I can tell there never has been a course taught on ecology at Fuller Seminary, where I teach.[127] This spring I advertised an elective course on the subject, but it had to be canceled due to low enrollment. Chris Accornero, a Ph.D. student in the Fuller School of World Mission, notes that in her recent survey of over 200 theological seminaries around the world, ecology did not even feature as an issue that needed to be addressed.[128]

This is not to say that the average seminary curriculum ignores social and political issues of all kinds. In the last two decades, as I have implied, there has been a growing awareness of the social and cultural contexts in which Christians preach the gospel. Poverty and injustice are issues to which many seminaries now give special attention.

For this we can be grateful. But why have our theological and missiological training practices ignored the realities highlighted in the recent Earth Summit in Río de Janeiro, Brazil? In the face of the mounting evidence of global warming, air and water pollution and so on, how does one account for this failure of vision?

While it is not possible to highlight all the factors here, we might note two.

The practical orientation of missiology

First, the practical orientation of missionaries and the focus on technique have all too often blinded them to larger contextual issues. Indeed, only in the last generation have missionaries begun to give serious attention to the cultural contexts in which mission work is carried out.[129]

This emphasis on contextualization has been an extremely important development in the history of missions and it has given us the tools with which we can address reflection on ecological problems. But by and large, missions has considered cultural concerns only as means to achieve the practical objectives of the missionary task—see the journal title "Practical Anthropology," for example—rather than as ends that are important in themselves.

One suspects that if we find that ecological concerns have a practical benefit in the evangelistic work of missions, we would find a way to include them in the curricula of our missions programs.

This practical orientation probably has deep roots in the Anglo-Saxon cultures from which most Western missionaries come.[130] But it also reflects underlying philosophical and theological commitments that characterize Western theology and that are inhospitable to ecological concerns. The author of this book makes some helpful comments on the individualism of American Christians. Surely this is a factor—not unrelated to the practical orientation I have noted above.

But the dichotomy between the spirit and the body that has been a part of theological reflection since the church's beginning in the Greco-Roman period probably plays a larger role. For centuries, Christians believed that God's primary concern was with the spirit, or as we have come to express it with the "human heart," which needs redemption from the limitations (and temptations) of bodily and earthly life. When this emphasis is present it is not hard to understand why environmental degradation issues are given short shrift.

The Christian story as historical project

A related emphasis has come to dominate theological reflection during the twentieth century: namely, the view that the Christian story is an essentially historical project. Christianity, as we have come to conceive it, is the story of God's involvement with creation and his love for the people he is calling to worship and serve him. Creation itself serves as a backdrop for this story, but we do not ordinarily see it as an actor in the story.

This story is thought to begin with God's calling of Abraham to go to a place to which he would direct him, and is accompanied by the promise that God would be the lord of this people. Theologians trace events through the history of Israel to the life and death of Jesus, culminating in the worship of God by his people in heaven.[131]

This has been an immensely important development in theology and there can be little doubt that it served to highlight elements of the biblical account that had previously gone unnoticed. In many ways it began to turn attention to this world as opposed to seeing our faith as primarily a matter of God and his people in heaven.

One of the gains of this turn to life in history was that issues of poverty and justice came to receive special attention. This is no small advance, and it deserves some emphasis. If the story of God involves a people called to reflect his goodness, then the *drama* of this story is clearly important to God.

Thanks to reflection done by our brothers and sisters in Latin America, we have seen ways in which salvation relates to the social and material life of people. It opened the door for putting together theologies of social justice and development. But in all this, we still saw the earth primarily as a setting for this human drama. Theologians did not give creation any independent theological importance. Clearly, the salvation-in-history framework did not stimulate a concern for the earth and its travail.[132]

Taking the "missiological revolution" further

Theological and missiological education then must address issues of justice as inherent in the gospel call. But it must now go further and insist that the earth and its resources are also of concern to God. Indeed, the theological reflection that supports such major changes—one is tempted to say such a revolution—has already begun.

We have already noticed that Christians have begun to conceive of missiology more holistically. The older wars over a "social gospel" have subsided and a consensus has emerged that the Good News includes people's social as well as their individual lives. This has led to a more wholesome understanding of the way development takes place and the interaction over time that this requires. Missiological education is already reflecting these changes.

But we must take the "missiological revolution" further. We must now understand that contextualism and holism include the plight of the earth and our responsibility to care for it. Indeed, we can no longer conceive of justice apart from this larger setting. How

145

can we understand the plight of the poor apart from desertification in Africa or the destruction of the rain forests in South America?[133]

Jurgen Moltmann has gone so far as to suggest in a recent book that this development marks a major shift in theology from its modern mode to a post-modern one—that is, from thinking of Christianity in relation to history, to understanding it in relation to nature.[134]

Charles Van Engen has suggested that what we need is a kingdom mission theology that would dramatically change the way we do mission, and we would add, the way we carry out missiological education. And this change may not be optional. He goes on to note, in perhaps the only reference I have come across in the missiological literature:

> The drastic ecological, economic, political, social, religious, demographic, and other changes happening in our small globe are presenting us with a new reality that will call for a new paradigm of theology of mission.[135]

It is encouraging to note that materials for the new paradigm are present. Important theological reflection is being done. But ironically the curriculum that we will use to train tomorrow's leaders has not yet come to reflect these changes. If such changes are not forthcoming, where will we find the men and women of vision for tomorrow's churches and mission agencies?

19

A missiological agenda for the twenty-first century

What have we learned on our tour of the environment? Several things:

1. First, a delicate balance between solar energy and matter is what makes life on earth sustainable. This is the secret of God's beautiful creation.

2. Humans can easily disrupt that equilibrium and push our planet into overload and disaster. In fact, this is exactly what has happened over the centuries of human existence on earth.

3. We can trace this destructive imbalance to sin—disobedience of God's commands, neglect of his assignments, failure to love and respect his creation, careless, greedy and inconsiderate use of the planet's resources.

4. The environmental crisis, perceived for many years by scientists, is no longer a series of local shortages and pollution. It is global and universal in its impact, calling for worldwide, international and concerted attention.

5. Like a complicated illness, ecological deterioration is difficult for anyone to comprehend, diagnose or

define, and its cure is even more elusive. But there are many things that we can do—some are being done already—to alleviate the earth's environmental sickness.

6. In the face of this challenge, the Christian church must recognize its need to build environmental awareness in its constituency, and to incorporate it in its worldwide mission.

7. From a missiological perspective, as is clearly articulated by our respondents, we Christians must be prepared to:

    7.1 Model a lifestyle of moderation and care of the poor, living as Jesus Christ would live among us today.

    7.2 Provide our development programs among those who are the poorest of the earth with ecological awareness and environmentally sound principles and actions.

    7.3 Recognize the biblically announced linkage between social justice and the fruitfulness of the earth and change the destructive policies, structures and practices that characterize our cultures and governments today.

    7.4 Incorporate into the training of our ministers, missionaries and church leaders an understanding of what Christian ecology is all about.

Watch . . . pray

One final exhortation—not from me, but from Christ himself:

Remembering that the Lord God is our Creator, and it is he who sustains all life by his Word, our responsibility is to "watch and pray"—watch for the signs of Christ's return and the end of the world, and pray for mercy and deliverance from the judgment it will represent.

When Jesus spoke to his disciples about the "wars . . . and famines and earthquakes in many places," as recorded in the Gospels, he added these words:

> *Just so, when you see all these things beginning to happen, you can know that my return is near, even at the doors. Then at last this age will come to its close. Heaven and earth will disappear, but my words remain forever (Matt. 24:33-35).*

We can expect a certain amount of incredulity and indifference from those around us. Noah's contemporaries, Jesus said, refused to believe that the great Flood was coming. And so it will be at the end of this age.

Scoffers abound today as they did in Noah's time. For example, in a "Global View" column in the *Wall Street Journal Europe*,[136] George Melloan quotes Vice President Albert Gore's remarks to the UN Earth Summit in Río de Janeiro, and compares them to the mysterious seven seals of the biblical book of the Revelation. "Theologians have for centuries puzzled over the book of Revelation's dramatic 'seven seals' prophecies," he states. "Al Gore's grim vision is easier to interpret. It's nonsense."

Melloan goes on to say that "Civilization is not destroying the planet. The only serious question is whether the U.S. vice president is just another scare monger or a man whose zealotry has deprived him of balanced and rational thought." According to Melloan, global warming, ozone depletion, loss of biodiversity, and so on, are myths—the phony science of "enviro-radicals."

As in every controversial issue, both sides can advance arguments—some of them valid, others wishful thinking. A former governor of Washington, for example, co-authored a book called *Environmental Overkill*.[137] Others sympathetic to corporate financial interests have been accused of trying to confuse the public by forming phony "green" fronts, such as the "Sahara Club" (obviously a parody of the well-known "Sierra Club") to promote their anti-environmental interests.

Comparing our present situation to Noah's day

Scoffers, as in the time of Noah, should not surprise us. We cannot expect anyone who is not a Christian to understand God's purposes in history—much less in future history. But comparisons with the Noahic experience, even to them, should be compelling.

God postponed the great Flood as long as he could. He did not want anyone to suffer extermination, but Noah's contemporaries refused to heed his warning. Today, likewise, the Apostle Peter says, God ". . . isn't really being slow about his promised return, even though it sometimes seems that way. But he is waiting, for the good reason that he is not willing that any should perish, and he is giving more time for sinners to repent" (2 Pet. 3:9).

This window of grace is our chance to get the gospel to the unevangelized of our society. "Remember why he is waiting," Peter reiterates. "He is giving us time to get his message of salvation out to others."

I like to interpret the history of Noah's day with a bit of plausible, but possibly imaginary, detail. It hinges on the character of Noah's great-grandfather, Enoch. After his son Methuselah was born, Enoch ". . . lived another 300 years in fellowship with God . . . then, when he was 365, and in constant touch with God, he disappeared, for God took him" (Gen. 5:22-24)!

It is not difficult to imagine that, like his ancestor Adam, Enoch walked and talked with God. The Lord God must have expressed to him his grief because of the wickedness of humankind and hinted about, or declared outright, his intention to ". . . blot out from the face of the earth all mankind that I created . . . for I am sorry I made them" (Gen. 6:7).

As we continue to reconstruct this imaginary conversation, we hear Enoch, frightened, questioning God, "When will that come to pass?" God points to Enoch's son and replied with what Hebrew scholars postulate as one of the possible meanings of Methuselah's name, "When he is gone, it will be."

So it may be more than coincidence that Methuselah died the same year the Flood came, and that he lived longer than any other person in human history. Judgment deferred was grace extended.

It has not been my purpose in this book to tell anybody how to live nor what to do. The path of responsibility will differ according to beliefs and circumstances. Each reader will have to search his or her own conscience—and to make this search habitual.

But our ecological excursion across these pages should at least have left us with a new awareness of how our planet is at risk because of excessive human impact and a new resolve to do what we can to help slow its demise.

Endnotes

Preface

1   Calvin B. DeWitt and Ghillean T. Prance, eds., *Missionary Earthkeeping* (Macon, Georgia: Mercer University Press, 1992), "Preface," p. viii. Reprinted with permission by Mercer University Press, Macon, GA 31207.

2   Ibid., p. 31. Luther Copeland, formerly a Southern Baptist missionary to Japan, is quoted by Dennis E. Testerman in his chapter entitled "Glimpses of the Past, Visions of the Future."

3   Tony Campolo, *How to Rescue the Earth without Worshiping Nature* (Nashville, Tennessee: Thomas Nelson Publishers, 1992), p. 5. Campolo made a similar statement while participating in a panel at a Christian Booksellers' convention in Dallas. He is quoted in *Publishers Weekly* (Sept. 21, 1992, p. 34) by William Griffin as saying:

> I've stood back and watched a whole generation lost to the Church because the Church refused to say anything about civil rights and the antiwar movement. I don't want to see that happen again. This is going to be the hot issue for the next generation, and I want the Church to be there in the forefront, saying what needs to be said. If kids are going to join the environmental movement, I want it to be a Christian bandwagon, not a New Age bandwagon.

4   DeWitt and Prance, *Missionary Earthkeeping*, "Introduction" by J. Mark Thomas, pp. 1, 2.

5   W. Dayton Roberts, *Running Out: A Compelling Look at the Current State of Planet Earth* (Ventura, California: Regal Book Division, G/L Publications, 1975).

PART I—BASICS
An Abbreviated Theology of the Environment

1—How the world works . . . and falters!

6   Al Gore, *Earth in the Balance: Ecology and the Human Spirit* (New York: Houghton Mifflin Company, 1992).

7   Calvin B. DeWitt, "Ethics, Ecosystems and Enterprise: Discovering the Meaning of Food Security and Development," *Growing Our Future: Food Security and the Environment*, Katie Smith and Tetsunao Yamamori, eds., (West Hartford, Connecticut: Kumarian Press, 1992), p. 10.

8   Paul Kennedy, *Preparing for the Twenty-First Century* (New York: Random House, 1993), p. 105.

9   This conclusion is convincingly argued in several World Vision publications and in chapter 16, "Population Growth and Human Development", of *UNEP 1992 Saving Our Planet: Challenges and Hopes* (Nairobi: UNEP, 1992), pp. 125-130. On page 130 the UNEP volume says:

> It has long been recognized—and particularly since the Stockholm Conference—that poverty is one of the greatest threats to the environment. In the developing countries, many choices that degrade the environment are made because of the imperative of immediate survival, not because of lack of concern for the future. Economic deprivation and environmental degradation have thus come to reinforce one another in a vicious cycle that perpetuates destitution in many developing countries. Top priority for the world community will have to be agreement on ways and means—many of them are well known—to stop this cycle.

10   UNEP, *Saving Our Planet*, p. 108.

2—What it would need to regain its balance

11   Ibid., p.105.

12   This evaluation is reinforced emphatically by Campolo, op. cit., in several passages, such as pp. 97, 112-119, 199.

13   Rachel Carson, *Silent Spring* (Boston: Houghton Mifflin, 1962).

14   Eugene P. Odum, 1970, quoted in a lecture at Fuller Theological Seminary, Pasadena, California (April 13, 1993) by Dr. C. T. Dyrness of Albany, Oregon. His (Odum's) was an early perception of the fact

that "man is faced with ultimate rather than regional limitations"—a perception he had reached "within the last two years."

15   Gore, *Earth in the Balance*, pp. 2, 3.

16   Paul Brand, "A Handful of Mud," originally presented at the Forum on the Theology of Creation, Institute of Environmental Studies, 1984, and published in the proceedings of the forum. Subsequently, it has appeared in *Christianity Today* (19 April, 1985: 26-27) and elsewhere.

17   See Notes, # 1, p. 23, at the close of DeWitt's chapter 1, "Ethics, Ecosystems and Enterprise: Discovering the Meaning of Food Security and Development," in Katie Smith and Tetsunao Yamamori, eds., *Growing Our Future*.

3—The way the Bible tells it

18   The biblical stories of creation and the Flood are found in the first chapters of the book of Genesis. Any direct quotations which appear here in the course of our paraphrased narration in this chapter are taken from *The Living Bible* and appear in italics. They are used with permission and identified by the references in parentheses.

4—Disasters are natural

19   Paul Harrison, *Inside the Third World* (Middlesex: England: Penguin Books, Middlesex, 1979 (1984).

5—Focusing on the future

6—A Christian environmentalist's creed

PART II—STATUS
Worrisome Holes, Threadbare Spots and Hopeful Patches

7—Population and pollution

20   *Earth Summit Report*, July 1, 1992. Prepared by the Environment and Natural Resources Group of the United Nations Development Programme (UNDP), courtesy of Fernando Zumbado J., Assistant Administrator and Regional Director for Latin America and the Caribbean.

21   Al Gore, *Earth in the Balance*, chapter 14, "A New Common Purpose," pp. 269-294.

22   David Hunt, *Global Peace and the Rise of Anti-Christ* (Eugene, Oregon: Harvest House, 1990), p. 163ff.

23   UNDP, *Earth Summit Report.*

24   UNEP, *Saving Our Planet.*

25   Loren Wilkinson, *Earthkeeping in the '90s* (Grand Rapids, Michigan: Eerdmans, 1980, 1991), p. 25.

26   Al Gore, *Earth in the Balance,* p. 31.

27   UNEP, *Saving Our Planet,* p. 125.

28   Ibid., p. 127.

29   Ibid., p. 1.

30   Ibid., p. 3.

31   Ibid., p. 10.

32   Ibid., p. 12.

33   Ibid., p. 102, chaps. 1, 10, 12.

34   Ibid., p. 78.

35   Ibid., pp. 111, 112.

8—Little drops of water—but too few?

36   Ibid., p. 33.

37   Sandra Postel, *Last Oasis: Facing Water Scarcity* (New York: W.W. Norton & Co., 1992), p. 27.

38   Ibid., p. 28.

39   UNEP, *Saving Our Planet,* p. 34.

40   Postel, *Last Oasis,* p. 49

41   Ibid., p. 50.

42   Ibid., p. 127.

43   Ibid., p. 129.

44   *Pasadena Star-News,* Pasadena, California, April 3, 1993.

45   UNEP, *Saving Our Planet,* p. 35.

46   Postel, *Last Oasis,* p. 10.

47   Ibid., p. 105.

9—Tracking our vanishing species

48   UNEP, *Saving Our Planet,* p. 53.

49   Ibid., p. 54.

50   Gore, *Earth in the Balance*, p. 24.

51   UNEP, *Saving Our Planet*, p. 54.

52   Ibid., p. 53.

53   Ibid., p. 54.

54   Ibid., p. 55.

55   Ibid., p. 56, Box 8.1.

10—Looking forward from Brazil

56   UNDP, *Earth Summit Report*. This "Earth Summit" report of the United Nations Development Programme (UNDP) has provided the data in large part for this chapter. Used with permission.

57   Diane Tegarden, "Several down-to-earth ways to help change the world," *Pasadena Star-News*, August 2, 1992.

11—Action plans and audits

58   Gore, *Earth in the Balance*, p. 295.

59   Ibid., pp. 305-307.

60   Ibid., pp. 182, 183.

61   Ibid., pp. 183-185.

62   Gil Friend, "Green Business" column, "Environmentalism good for the bottom line," *Pasadena Star-News*, July 20, 1992.

63   Idem, "Environmental clean-up figures in the bottom line," *Pasadena Star-News*, August 17, 1992.

64   Ibid.

12—The case of the conscientious CEO

65   James J. MacKenzie, *Driving Forces: Motor Vehicle Trends and Their Implications for Global Warming, Energy Strategies and Transportation Planning*, (Washington: World Resources Institute, 1990).

66   UNEP, *Saving Our Planet*, p. 116.

67   Ibid., pp. 116-119.

68   *Time*, Technology, "Off and Humming," April 26, 1993, p. 53.

69   UNEP, *Saving Our Planet*, p. 110.

70   Gore, *Earth in the Balance*, pp. 92-95.

71   While Gore and many others insist on the validity of a global warming trend and on the need to act before it gets worse, and hence irre-

versible, other scientists are more cautious and claim that the evidence is not yet incontrovertible. A recent seminar in Long Beach, CA, highlighted several perspectives:

> (1) All agree that a "greenhouse effect" is a natural process that traps the sun's warmth in the atmosphere. They disagree about whether burning fossil fuels adds substantially to the problem.

> (2) Temperature readings in the 1800's were not so accurate as those in today's computerized science. Trends, therefore, may be misleading or exaggerated.

> (3) The real debate is over how drastically and how urgently the apparent risks should be addressed. (See Steve Scauzillo, "Evidence not in, jury's still out on greenhouse effect, scientists say," *Pasadena Star-News*, June 6, 1993.)

72   These data and subsequent information in the rest of this chapter are taken from newspaper clippings, news releases and comments furnished by the staff of AES Corporation. The text was then submitted to Dennis Bakke, who penned in some minor revisions and gave permission for publication. We are most grateful to him and to his staff for their cooperation.

13—A fraternity of missionary earthkeepers

73   Ghillean T. Prance, chapter 2, "The Ecological Awareness of the Amazon Indians," *Missionary Earthkeeping*, DeWitt and Prance, eds., pp. 49, 50.

74   Calvin DeWitt, Case Four, "Missionary Earthkeeping," *Growing Our Future*, Smith and Yamamori, eds., p. 138.

75   Ibid., p. 136.

76   Prance, *Missionary Earthkeeping*, p. 47.

77   Dennis Testerman, chapter 1, "Glimpses of the Past, Visions of the Future," *Missionary Earthkeeping*, pp. 24, 25.

78   Ibid., p. 26.

79   Ibid., p. 21.

80   Ibid., p. 30.

81   Calvin DeWitt, "Introduction," *Missionary Earthkeeping*, pp. 7-9.

82   Fr. Robert Clobus, chapter 3, "Ecofarming and Land Ownership in Ghana," *Missionary Earthkeeping*, p. 63ff. This address has also appeared in *Together*, the journal of World Vision International, and in W. Dayton Roberts, ed., *Africa: A Season for Hope* (Ventura: Cali-

fornia: Regal Books, GL Publications, 1985).

14—Countdown

83   Dennis L. Meadows, et al, *The Limits to Growth: A Report for the Club of Rome's Project on the Predicament of Mankind* (New York: Universe Books, 1972); and Club of Rome, "Mankind at the Turning Point," quoted by *Time*, October 21, 1974.

84   UNEP, *Saving Our Planet*, p. 125ff.

85   Ibid., p. 33ff.

86   Ibid., p. 25ff.

87   Ibid., p. 1ff.

88   Lauran Neergaard, "164 Million Americans suffer from polluted air," *Pasadena Star-News*, April 30, 1993.

89   UNEP, *Saving Our Planet*, p. 44ff.

90   Ibid., p. 47ff.

91   Ibid., p. 53ff.

92   Ibid., p. 99ff. and p. 59ff.

PART III—REACTIONS
Pressure Points in the Christian Mission

15—Walking lightly on the earth
Dwayne Hodgson and Ron Sider

93   Ronald J. Sider, "Green Theology," *ESA Advocate* (Wynnewood, Pennsylvania: Evangelicals for Social Action, July/August 1991), p. 2.

94   Wesley Granberg-Michaelson, *A Worldly Spirituality: The Call to Redeem Life on Earth* (San Francisco: Harper & Row Publishers, 1984), pp. 61 & 65.

95   RSV (Revised Standard Version) is cited here. Nature is linked in this passage with the "sons of God" who will experience resurrection from the dead.

96   Tony Campolo, *How to Rescue the Earth*, 1992, p. 96.

97   This interpretation reflects a more inclusive definition of salvation that incorporates both people and the created world. For example, to our Western ears, John 3:16 has often been heard as an expression of God's desire to redeem the fallen human "world." While this is certainly true, recent biblical interpretation suggests that the Greek

159

word which is usually translated as "world" (*cosmos*) includes all of creation as well (Granberg-Michaelson, 1984, p. 116).

98   Granberg-Michaelson, 1984, p. 86.

99   Sider, 1991, p. 4.

100 Ronald J. Sider, *Rich Christians in an Age of Hunger* (Dallas & Vancouver: Word Publishing, 1990).

101 Ibid, p. 129.

102 As well, there is the problem that environmentalism remains largely a middle class issue, the luxury of those who have the time and resources to pursue it. Yet poverty and environmental issues are clearly interrelated, and must be addressed a such. The inner city neighborhood with the toxic waste dump is as much a part of the environment as the old-growth forest threatened by clear cutting. We must be careful that we do not fall into a romantic idealization of ecology that only benefits those who can afford to vacation in the wilderness.

103 Sider, *Rich Christians*, p. 123.

104 Granberg-Michaelson, *A Worldly Spirituality*, p. 95; Sider, *Rich Christians*, p. 143.

105 Campolo, *How to Rescue the Earth*, p. 199.

106 Doris Janzen Longacre, *Living More with Less* (Waterloo, Ontario, and Scottsdale, PA: Herald Press, 1980), p. 25; Sider, *Rich Christians*, p. 147.

107 Campolo, *How to Rescue the Earth*, p. 199.

108 Ibid.

109 Ibid., p. 198. Please note: this is not to propose "Green Christianity" as a prerequisite of our salvation—for salvation clearly is by grace—rather, living an environmentally sustainable lifestyle is a product of our redemption and obedience to the Creator and Redeeming God whom we serve.

110 E. F. Schumacher, *Small is Beautiful: Economics as if People Mattered* (New York: Harper & Row, 1973).

111 These assumptions are what Jacques Ellul terms the "sacreds" of society—the unquestioned foundational beliefs that frame most of our decisions and actions (1964).

112 Batteries offer a telling example of "green-wash" marketing. Many major producers of disposable batteries offer a "cleaner" alternative product line that contains a smaller percentage of heavy metals but

retails for a higher price. While this reform is laudable, the same companies continue to produce the cheaper, more hazardous batteries in an effort to capture the lower-priced market share. Unless the companies intend to phase out these more toxic lines, the green alternative would appear to be simply another example of product differentiation aimed at maximizing profits.

113   Living in the suburbs offers a good example. In many large, Canadian cities, living downtown is out of the price range of many middle class families, and they must live in suburban homes. These subdivision designs assume that everyone has access to a car, and hence essential services and jobs are often located a fair distance away. Even if people want to reduce their reliance on automobiles, the lack of convenient public transit necessitates car travel, and the sheer volume of automobile traffic combined with the distance makes bicycle commuting impossible for most people. An ecologically feasible alternative would be to design new subdivisions within walking distance of community stores and job sites, and with ample public transit and bicycle paths.

114   Longacre, *Living More with Less*, pp. 56-59.

115   Sider, *Rich Christians*, p. 202.

116   Longacre, *Living More with Less*, p. 47.

117   Tony Campolo and Gordon Aeschliman, *50 Ways You Can Help Save the Planet* (Downers Grove, Illinois: InterVarsity Press, 1992).

118   This was the case at McMaster University in Hamilton, Ontario. In the late 1980s, a small group of students took the initiative to start a campus recycling program for cans and bottles, despite protests from the university administration that it was too expensive. After running the program through volunteers and lobbying the administration, the university eventually undertook the project itself. A similar experience took place at Biola University in California.

119   Campolo & Aeschliman, *50 Ways You Can Help*, pp. 15-36.

120   A note of warning: When purchasing recycled products, make sure you check to see the percentage of "post-consumer" products that are included. Paper manufacturers, for example, can include "pre-consumer" by-products and classify the product as "recycled." This isn't necessarily a bad practice, as it eliminates production wastes. However, it does little to reabsorb the outflow from consumers or to reduce the extraction of raw materials from the eco-system.

121   Campolo, *How to Rescue the Earth*, p. 198.

16—Patching garments . . . patching communities
Stephen K. Commins

122 Siobahn Mellon, "Permaculture in Nepal," *Food Matters* (April 1993).

123 Robert Chambers, *Sustainable Livelihoods, Environment and Development*, Institute of Development Studies, Sussex, England, December 1987.

124 Ibid., p. 6.

125 Peter Cormack, "Finding the Natural, Enduring Balance," *Together* (July-September 1991).

126 John Steward, "Sustaining the Change Process," *Together* (July-September 1991).

17—Global justice and the environment
Job Ebenezer

18—Training missionary earthkeepers
William Dyrness

127 I understand that the environmental crisis is touched upon in a course on Christian Development which is offered by Fuller's School of World Mission, and possibly in other courses as well, but my statement still stands.

128 See her unpublished study, *Issues in Missiological Education* (1993) Fuller School of World Mission. She asked these institutions: "What are the main issues in missiological education today for your particular part of the world?" or "in the development of mission leaders?" As might be expected, responses focused on issues of contextualization and integration in missions, though holistic mission and socio-political concerns were also expressed. The closest thing to an ecological concern was the desire for practical courses in African institutions: cattle projects, dry land agriculture and carpentry.

Dennis E. Testerman has pointed out, however, that outside the evangelical movement attention has been given to this by Asian theologians meeting in 1977. They stated that in some seminaries "there is already an attempt to relate theology to life in nature by the inclusion of agriculture in the curriculum." (*Missionary Earthkeeping*, DeWitt and Prance, eds., p. 30).

129 One of the first serious studies of this kind was Eugene Nida's *Customs and Cultures* (New York: Harper and Row, 1954). This vision was carried out by the journal *Practical Anthropology* (1952-1971). See

on this whole subject Charles R. Taber, *The World Is Too Much with Us: "Culture" in Modern Protestant Missions* (Macon, Georgia: Mercer University Press, 1991).

130   I have argued this in my book, *How Does America Hear the Gospel?* (Grand Rapids, Michigan: Eerdmans, 1989), see especially chapter 3.

131   Many works reflect this emphasis, but one of the most influential has been G. E. Wright, *The God Who Acts* (London: SCM, 1953). See also Oscar Cullmann, *Salvation in History* (New York: Harper and Row, 1968).

132   The first person to make this point in any complete way was Jurgen Moltmann in *God in Creation* (San Francisco: Harper and Row, 1986). See the important survey in H. Paul Santmire, *The Travail of Nature: The Ambiguous Ecological Promise of Christian Theology* (Philadelphia: Fortress Press, 1985).

133   See Paul Harrison, *Inside the Third World* (Penguin, 1979).

134   See *The Way of Jesus Christ* (San Francisco: Harper and Row, 1991).

135 See *The Good News of the Coming Kingdom*, Charles Van Engen, Dean Gilliland and Paul Pierson, eds., (Maryknoll, N.Y.: Orbis, 1993), p. 259. Other resources pointing to this paradigm shift are Calvin DeWitt and Ghillean T. Prance, eds., *Missionary Earthkeeping*; and the *Evangelical Review of Theology*, Vol.17, No. 2. April 1993, a special issue on "Evangelicals and the Environment."

19—A missionary agenda for the twenty-first century

136   *Wall Street Journal Europe*, Tuesday, July 13, 1993.

137   Dixie Lee Ray & Lou Guzzo, *Environmental Overkill: Whatever Happened to Common Sense?* (Regnery Gateway, 1993).

Index

 **MARC**

Bringing you key resources on the world mission of the church

MARC books and other pulications support the work of MARC (Mission Advanced Research and Communications Center),which is to inspire fresh vision and empower the Christian mission among those whe extend the whole gospel to the whole world.

Recent MARC titles include:

▶ *Bridging the Gap: Evangelism, Development and Shalom* by Bruce Bradshaw. The author uses the biblical concept of *Shalom* to bridge the gaps between evangelism and development when we perceive them as separate enterprises of Christian mission. $11.95

▶ *Mission Handbook 1993-95*. The 1993-95 edition continues as the most comprehensive listing available of Christian mission agencies based in North America, with detailed up-to-date descriptions and statistics, analyses and essays. Also available in a powerful IBM-compatible computer software version.

   Mission Handbook plus *Mission Handbook on Disk*. . $119.95
   Mission Handbook on Disk (software only). . . . . $ 99.95
   Mission Handbook 1993-95 (book only). . . . . $ 39.95

▶ *The Changing Shape of World Mission* by Bryant L. Myers. Presents in color graphs, charts and maps the challenge before missions globally, including the unfinished task of world evangelization. Also available in color slides and over-heads—excellent for presentations.

   Book. . . . .$ 5.95
   Slides. . . . . $ 99.95
   Overheads. . . . . $ 99.95
   Presentation Set *(one book, slides and overheads)* $175.00

▶ *Women as Leaders* by Katherine Haubert. Scrutinizes Scripture to help the reader come to his or her own conclusions about the contemporary reality of women leaders in the church and ministry. Formatted to facilitate easy group or individual study. $8.95

▶ *I Sing of Hope* by Valdir R. Steuernagel. A Latin American examines Psalm 146 in tandem with Mary's *Magnificat* and invites the reader to transform the passages into a program of action. $4.95

Order Toll Free in USA: 1-800-777-7752
Visa and MasterCard accepted

▶**MARC** A division of World Vision International
121 E. Huntington Dr. • Monrovia • CA • 91016-3400

Ask for the MARC Newsletter and complete publications list